Trace-Element Analyses of Core Samples from the 1967–1988 Drillings of Kilauea Iki Lava Lake, Hawaii

By Rosalind Tuthill Helz

Open-File Report 2012–1050

U.S. Department of the Interior
U.S. Geological Survey

U.S. Department of the Interior
KEN SALAZAR, Secretary

U.S. Geological Survey
Marcia K. McNutt, Director

U.S. Geological Survey, Reston, Virginia: 2012

For more information on the USGS—the Federal source for science about the Earth,
its natural and living resources, natural hazards, and the environment—visit
http://www.usgs.gov or call 1–888–ASK–USGS

For an overview of USGS information products, including maps, imagery, and publications,
visit *http://www.usgs.gov/pubprod*

To order this and other USGS information products, visit *http://store.usgs.gov*

Suggested citation:
Helz, R.T., 2012, Trace-element analyses of core samples from the 1967–1988 drillings of
Kilauea Iki lava lake, Hawaii: U.S. Geological Survey Open-File Report 2012–1050, 46 p.,
available only at *http://pubs.usgs.gov/of/2012/1050.*

Contents

Figures

Tables

Conversion Factors

Inch/Pound to SI

Multiply	By	To obtain
foot (ft)	0.3048	meter (m)

SI to Inch/Pound

Multiply	By	To obtain
meter (m)	3.281	foot (ft)

Temperature in degrees Celsius (°C) may be converted to degrees Fahrenheit (°F) as follows:
°F=(1.8×°C)+32

Trace-Element Analyses of Core Samples from the 1967–1988 Drillings of Kilauea Iki Lava Lake, Hawaii

By Rosalind Tuthill Helz

Introduction

This report presents previously unpublished analyses of trace elements in drill core samples from Kilauea Iki lava lake and from the 1959 eruption that fed the lava lake. The two types of data presented were obtained by instrumental neutron-activation analysis (INAA) and energy-dispersive X-ray fluorescence analysis (EDXRF). The analyses were performed in U.S. Geological Survey (USGS) laboratories from 1989 to 1994. This report contains 93 INAA analyses on 84 samples and 68 EDXRF analyses on 68 samples. The purpose of the study was to document trace-element variation during chemical differentiation, especially during the closed-system differentiation of Kilauea Iki lava lake.

Background and Previous Work

Kilauea Iki lava lake formed during the 1959 eruption of Kilauea Volcano, when lava ponded in the previously existing Kilauea Iki pit crater (located just east of the summit caldera, see fig. 1). The eruption was well documented and extensively sampled, and 23 samples of 1959 eruption material were analyzed by Murata and Richter (1966). Wright (1973) and Helz (1987a) have demonstrated and quantified the role of magma mixing during this eruption, using the bulk chemical data of Murata and Richter (1966), plus mineral and glass chemistry obtained using the electron microprobe.

Kilauea Iki lava lake remained accessible throughout the period of its cooling and crystallization (from 1959 to the mid-1990s) and therefore has been drilled repeatedly; the earliest core, recovered in 1960–1962, was described by Richter and Moore (1966). Subsequent drilling was carried out in 1967, 1975, 1976, 1979, 1981, and 1988. The locations of the resulting drill holes are shown in plan view in figure 2 and in cross section in figure 3. Further details on the later drilling episodes, plus petrographic logs of the cores, are given in Helz and others (1984) for the 1967–1979 cores, in Helz and Wright (1983) for the 1981 cores, and in Helz (1993) for the 1988 cores.

1

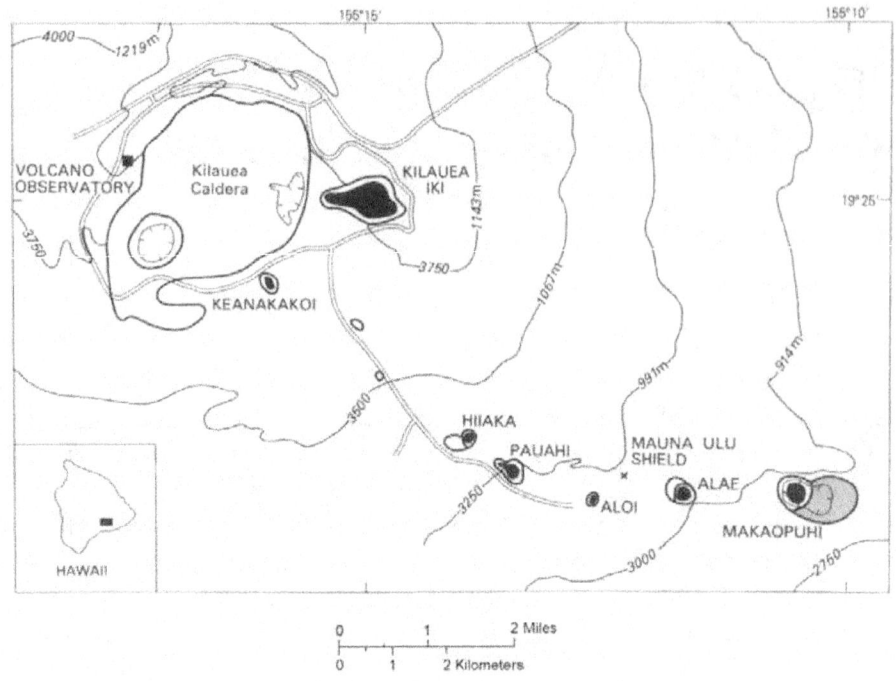

Contour Interval 250 Feet = 76 Meters

Figure 1. Index map of the summit area of Kilauea Volcano. All historical lava lakes formed to date (1994) are shown in black. The prehistoric Makaopuhi lava lake is shown in the gray, stippled pattern. The historical lava lakes in Aloi, Alae, and Makaopuhi pit craters are now covered by lavas from the Mauna Ulu satellite shield, the summit of which is indicated by the "X".

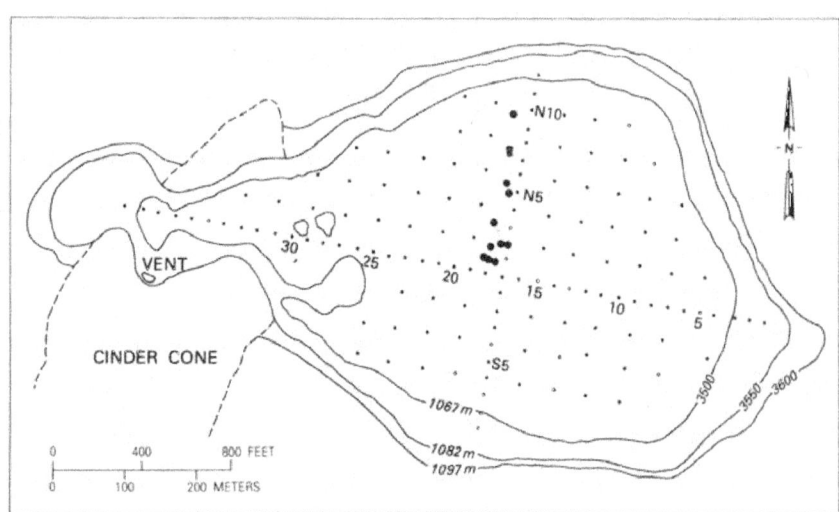

Figure 2. Plan view of the post-1959 surface of Kilauea Iki. The lake surface has a network of leveling stations, the locations of which are shown by the small dots. Larger dots indicate the locations of holes drilled from 1967 to 1988.

2

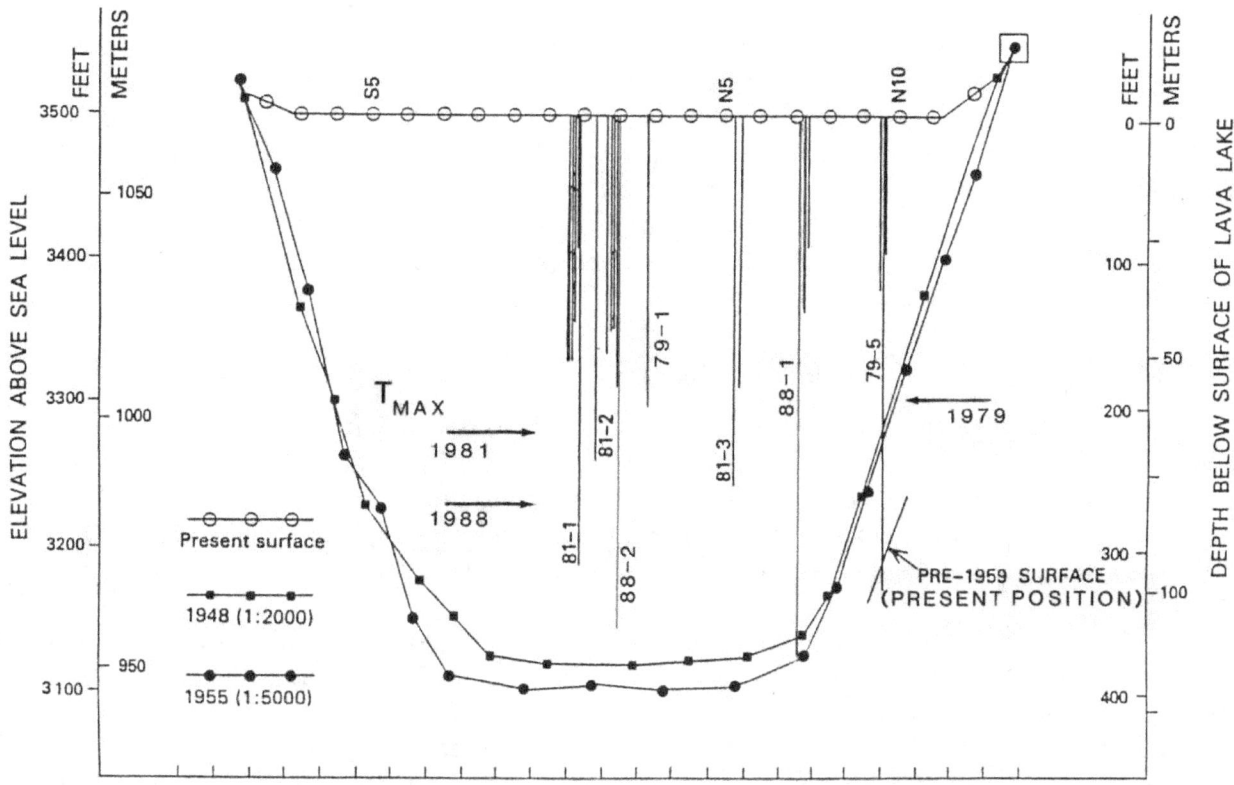

Figure 3. Cross section of Kilauea Iki lava lake taken along the central line of closely spaced levelling stations shown in figure 2. The present surface of the lava lake and two pre-eruption profiles are shown; they are joined at the square (upper right). The two pre-eruption profiles are taken from two different topographic maps: one (at 1:2,000) is based on aerial photographs taken in 1948; the other (at 1:5,000) is based on aerial photographs taken in 1955. Both maps were prepared by R. Jordan, U.S. Geological Survey, Flagstaff, Arizona. The present position of the lake bottom has been intersected only at the location of drill hole KI79-5 and lies 20 to 23 meters deeper here and across the flat central floor than the pre-eruptive topography would suggest. Vertical exaggeration is 4:1.

The drill holes are shown as vertical lines projected onto this cross section. Several of the drill hole locations have been reoccupied more than once, in order to sample the same section of the crust in several stages of development. Spacing between these closely spaced holes is not to scale in this figure. Only the deepest hole in each cluster has been labeled, for clarity. The arrows mark the position of the thermal maximum in 1979, 1981, and 1988, as determined by analyzing glass in quenched, partially molten drill core using the glass geothermometer of Helz and Thornber (1987).

Kilauea Iki cores have been studied extensively, including petrography and microprobe analysis of individual phases, plus chemical analysis of bulk samples. The results of studies based on the 1967–1981 cores were reported in Helz (1980; 1987a, b), Helz and Thornber (1987), Helz and others (1989), Helz and others (1994), and Barth and others (1994). Helz (2009) was the first paper to make use of the major-element analytical results for the 1988 core, which were presented in Helz and Taggart (2010).

There have been few prior reports on the trace-element compositions of core from the lava lake, with the notable exception of a study by Pitcher and others (2009) of the platinum-group elements and Re in a suite of 14 samples from Kilauea Iki plus 5 from the 1959 eruption. The 1959 eruption pumices, by contrast, have been analyzed for various trace elements twice previously, by Gunn (1971) and by Tilling and others (1987). The results reported here will be compared with those of the earlier studies.

Sample Selection and Analytical Methods

After 242 Kilauea Iki samples had been analyzed for major elements (Helz and others, 1994; Helz and Taggart, 2010), the present subset of 84 was submitted for trace-element analysis. Samples for trace-element analysis were chosen to represent all rock types found in the lake and the full range of major-element compositional variation observed. In order to obtain data for a large suite of trace elements of varying geochemical behavior, the samples were submitted for both INAA and EDXRF analysis.

The INAA analyses were obtained between 1989 and 1994; the samples were irradiated at the USGS TRIGA reactor in Denver, Colorado, and analyzed in the USGS Radiochemistry Laboratory in Reston, Virginia. The general INAA procedure is described in Baedecker and McKown (1987), and the data reduction techniques are given in Grossman and Baedecker (1987) and Baedecker and Grossman (1989). Eighty-five samples were analyzed over the period from 1989 to 1994. This procedure generates values for a number of elements found in the major-element analyses, as well as approximately 27 trace elements. Of the elements normally reported as majors (Na, K, Ca, Ti, Cr, and Fe), only the values for Cr have been included in the tables in this report. All data were generated by the standard methods as described except for the Cs values for job CE96, which were recounted 525 days after irradiation in order to obtain better values. The analysts were J.N. Grossman and P.A. Baedecker.

The EDXRF analyses were performed in 1992 in the USGS analytical laboratory in Menlo Park, California. The EDXRF procedure is that of Johnson and King (1987). Elements requested included Ni, Cu, and Zn, which were fluoresced with a germanium target, and Rb, Sr, Y, Zr, and Nb, fluoresced with a silver target. Ba, La, and Ce analyses, which would have required a different target, were not requested. The analyst was J. Kent.

In order to evaluate the observed variation of Zn in the lava lake samples, it was necessary to obtain some data for Zn in olivines. These data were obtained on the JEOL electron microprobe (Reston, Va.). The usual olivine standardization package (including Si, Fe, Mg, Ca, Mn, Ni, Al, Ti, and Cr) was expanded to include Zn. Counting times used for Zn were 180 seconds (on peak) and 90 seconds both above and below the peak (for background), in order to obtain reasonably stable counts. The modified package was set up by Harvey Belkin (USGS), whose assistance is greatly appreciated.

Description of the Analytical Tables

Tables of analytical data are presented at the end of this report. Table A1 presents INAA data for the 1959 eruption samples, while tables A2–A6 present INAA data for the 1967, 1975, 1979, 1981, and 1988 core samples. Table B1 includes the EDXRF data for the 1959 eruption samples, and tables B2–5 include the results for the 1967, 1975, 1979, and 1981 samples. No EDXRF analyses were obtained for the 1988 core samples.

Each sample is identified by a field number. For the 1959 samples (in tables A1 and B1), these are of the form "Iki-1" and correspond to numbers given by scientists observing the 1959 eruption. Entries under "Lab no." of the form "S-1" correspond to designations given in table 1 of Murata and Richter (1966). The analysis of Iki-3 was presented in Helz and Taggart (2010), and the lab number is the one for the major-element analysis.

For the samples from the lava lake (tables A2–A6 and B2–B5), the field number is of the form "67-1-89.0," where the first number gives the year the sample was drilled (1967), the second is the number of the drill hole within the year (1), and the third is the depth from which the sample was recovered (in this case 89.0 feet). For these samples, the "Lab. no." is a number assigned for purposes of sample control within the USGS analytical laboratory system. In all cases, this number corresponds to the number for the major-element analysis, as given in Helz and others (1994) or Helz and Taggart (2010). These are usually not the same as individual lab numbers in the trace-element analytical jobs. The next line shows the job numbers for the trace elements. The INAA data include job numbers CD53, CE76, CE92, CG74, CJ12, and CJ13. The EDXRF data are from jobs CH90 and CH91.

Concentration data for trace elements are reported as given in the internal reports. The INAA reports included the 1-sigma analytical uncertainty from counting statistics, but those numbers are not repeated here. Estimates of precision are given in Baedecker and McKown (1987). All concentrations are in parts per million except for Au, which is given in parts per billion. Entries shown as "<" indicate concentrations below the limit of detection, while "nd" means that the element was not determined for that sample in the particular analytical job.

In all cases, the tables include the bulk MgO content of the samples, as reported in Murata and Richter (1966), Helz and others (1994) and Helz and Taggart (2010). Additional information on each sample is provided below the analyses. For the 1959 eruption samples, tables A1 and B1 also give the phase of the eruption, the fraction of juvenile magma present in the sample (Wright, 1973) and the quenching temperature of the glass present in the sample (Helz, 1987a). For samples from the lava lake (tables A2–A6 and B2–B5), the first of the lower entries repeats descriptions of the samples as given in Helz and others (1994) and Helz and Taggart (2010). The Roman numerals give the zone numbers where defined [Helz and others (1989); Helz and Taggart (2010)]. The zonation pattern is shown in figure 4.

The tables also note whether the sample analyzed contains glass (= quenched melt) or not. Lastly, the core has been put into one of three categories, depending on its pre-quenching temperature. "High" samples are those quenched from temperatures above the solidus, which lies at 970 to 980°C; these contain glass interpreted as having been a stable melt phase prior to quenching. "Medium" samples are those quenched from temperatures below the solidus but above the boiling point of water (approximately 110°C for the geothermal system in the lake, as the water contains some dissolved salts). "Low" temperature samples are those that were quenched from 110°C and hence had been in contact with liquid water (which contained some dissolved salts, mainly Na_2SO_4) prior to drilling. This information is included because it bears on the freshness of the material analyzed, though all Kilauea Iki core is pristine by normal geologic standards.

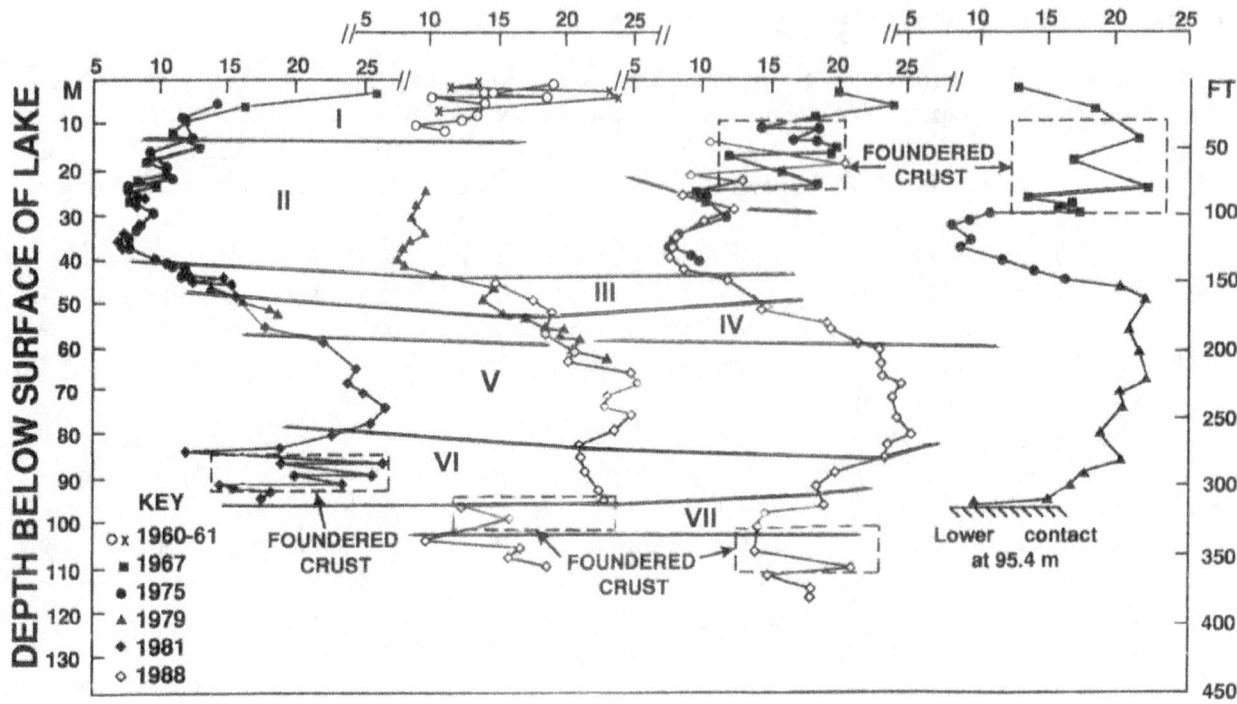

Figure 4. MgO content (weight percent) of olivine-phyric core versus depth below the surface of Kilauea Iki lava lake, modified from figure 3 in Helz (2009). Zone boundaries, as defined by the results of Helz and others (1994) and Helz and Taggart (2010), are shown and the enclosed areas labeled.

Availability and Coherence of Trace-Element Data

This section reviews the coherence of the trace-element data, first within the new data presented here and then among the three sets of analyses available for the 1959 eruption samples (this study; Gunn, 1971; and Tilling and others, 1987). Table 1 summarizes the availability of data and methods used in these various studies and shows that two to four kinds of data are available for 16 of the 23 elements. Elements listed in only one column are As, Se, Sb, Ta, Au, and Th (INAA only) and Nb (EDXRF only); of these only Nb, Ta, and Th are consistently above the limit of detection in these samples.

Comparisons Within This Study

Five elements (Ni, Zn, Rb, Sr, and Zr) are reported in both the INAA and EDXRF tables. In addition, there are two sets of Cr data, the INAA data reported here and the values reported with the major-element analyses (Helz and others, 1994; Helz and Taggart, 2010) or, for the 1959 eruption samples, in Wright (1973). These data are compared in figures 5 and 6 below.

Table 1. Elements analyzed, by method or by study.

[INAA, instrumental neutron-activation analysis; EDXRF, energy-dispersive X-ray fluorescence analysis;"X" indicates element concentrations in agreement with at least one other set of analytical data; "x" indicates inconsistent results or only one data set]

Element	This study INAA	This study EDXRF	Tilling and others (1987) INAA	Tilling and others (1987) other*	Gunn (1971) XRF
Sc	X		X		
Cr	X		X		X
Co	X		X		x-high
Ni	X	X		x-low	X
Zn	x-low	X		x-high	X
Cu		x			x
As	x				
Se	x				
Rb	X	X			x-low
Sr	x-some high	X	x-some low		X
Y		x		X	x
Zr	x	x			
Mo	x			X	
Sb	x				
Cs	x		x		
Ba	X		X		X
REE	X (8)		X (8)		
Hf	X		X		
Nb		x			
Ta	x				
Au	x				
Th	x				
U	X			X	
Other				V, Ga, Pb	Ga

*Emission spectroscopy except for U, which was done by fission track counting.

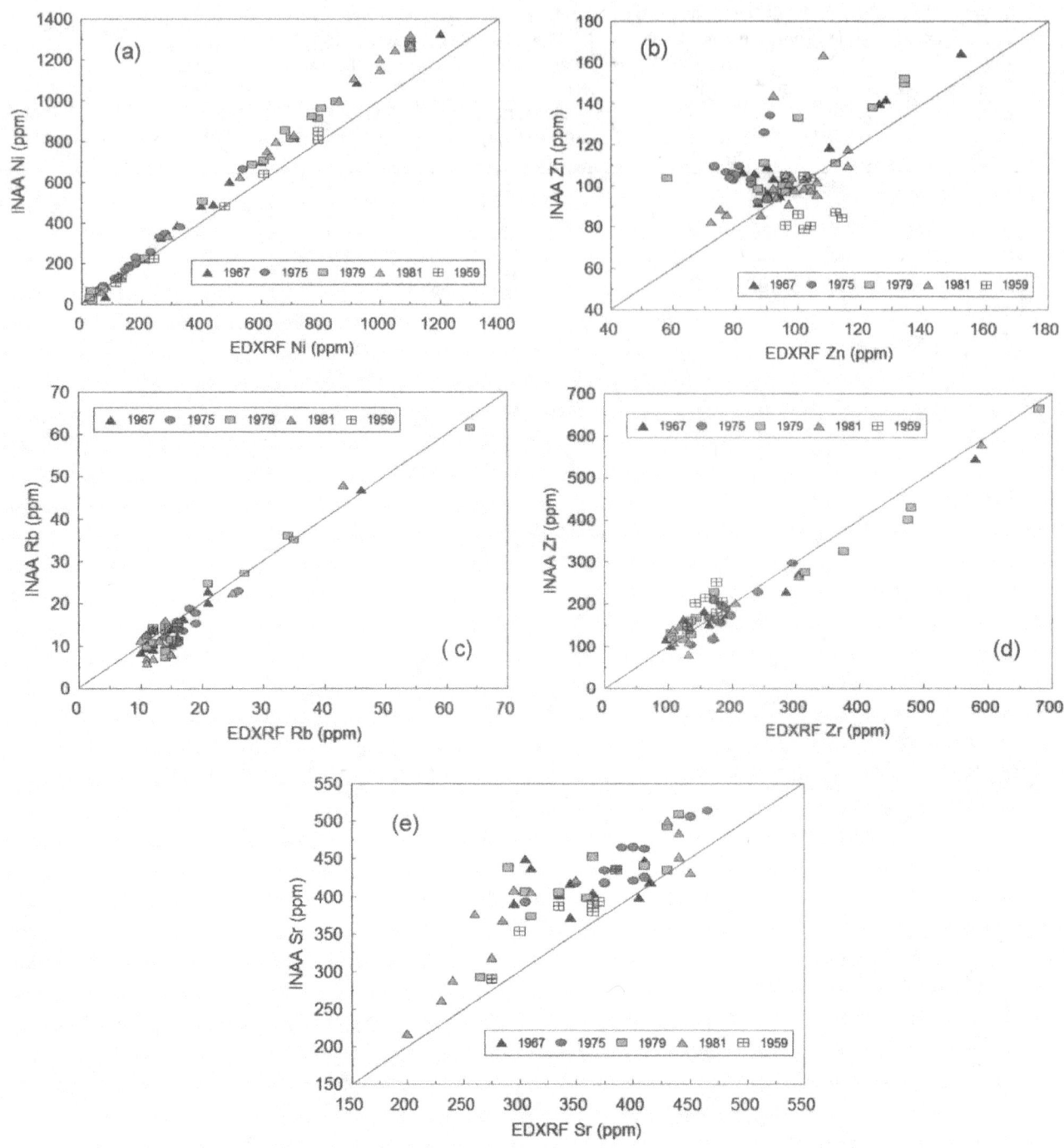

Figure 5. Plots comparing instrumental neutron-activation analysis (INAA) and energy-dispersive X-ray fluorescence (EDXRF) data for five elements from the present study. All quantities are in parts per million (ppm).

Figures 5a and 5b compare INAA and EDXRF values for Ni and Zn, which are highly or mildly compatible with olivine. Ni concentrations are co-linear, with the INAA values mostly falling slightly above the 1:1 line, except for data from job CE92. By contrast, Zn data correlate very poorly; it is not clear from this plot which set gives the more satisfactory values for Zn.

Figures 5c, 5d, and 5e show how Rb, Zr and Sr compare between the two analytical methods. The two highly incompatible elements (Rb, Zr) fall relatively close to the 1:1 line over a large range of concentrations, while the data for Sr correlate rather poorly, with the INAA values consistently higher than the EDXRF data.

Figure 6 shows that when INAA values for Cr are plotted against determinations for Cr_2O_3 included in earlier reports (Wright, 1973; Helz and others, 1994; Helz and Taggart, 2010), the data fall in a broad linear array. The data on older (1967–1981) cores and the 1959 samples were obtained colorimetrically (Kirschenbaum, 1983) or by flame atomic absorption (Aruscavage and Crock, 1987), as described in Helz and others (1994). They are consistent with each other and with the INAA analyses. The Cr_2O_3 data for the 1988 samples, which were obtained by inductively coupled plasma atomic emission spectroscopy (Lichte and others, 1987), tend to be high.

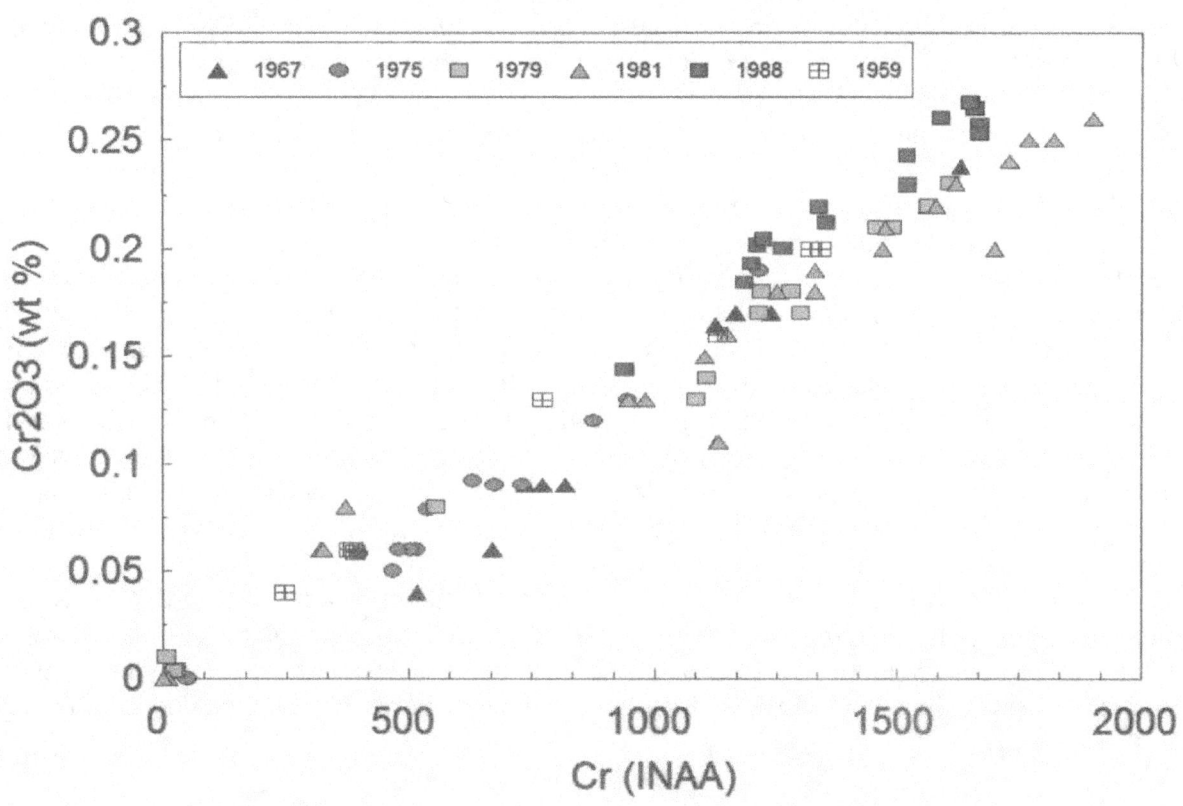

Figure 6. Cr_2O_3 values (weight percent) plotted against instrumental neutron-activation analysis (INAA) determinations for Cr in parts per million for all samples in the present study.

Comparisons Among the 1959 Eruption Samples

The 1959 summit eruption of Kilauea has been studied intensively for many years (Murata and Richter, 1966; Wright, 1973; Helz, 1987a), and some samples from the eruption were previously analyzed for trace elements by Gunn (1971) and Tilling and others (1987), as summarized in table 1. This section will use these results plus the new data to evaluate the results in the context of what is known about the petrology of the 1959 eruption samples.

The 1959 eruption was picritic, with most samples consisting of vesicular brown glass and varying amounts of olivine and chromite (Richter and Murata, 1966; Helz, 1987a). The trace-element variations reflect this limited crystalline assemblage, as discussed in Gunn (1971). Thus all samples would be expected to fall on straight lines in magnesia variation diagrams (Wright, 1971; Wright, 1973).

Figures 7a and 7b show how element concentrations for Ni and Co (fig. 7a) and Zn (fig. 7b) vary as a function of MgO content. These divalent cations enter olivine to varying extents: Ni is strongly compatible, decreasing markedly as bulk MgO content (and hence olivine phenocryst content) decreases. Three of four analytical sets have similar Ni values; those of Tilling and others (1987), made in the developmental phase of the INAA technique, run low at higher MgO contents. Co decreases slightly but perceptibly as MgO decreases, while Zn is so noisy it is not clear whether the slope is positive or negative. Of the four data sets, those of Gunn (1971) and the EDXRF data of the present study are in agreement with each other, suggesting that these are the best values available.

Figures 7c–e show how the concentrations of six elements incompatible with olivine vary as a function of MgO content in the 1959 samples. The concentration of these elements increases as MgO decreases, as would be expected. In figure 7c, the Sr data are somewhat noisy, with the Gunn (1971) and the EDXRF data showing the least scatter. Two (of four) Sr points from Tilling and others (1987) are in good agreement with the other sets, but the two less magnesian samples run low, confirming the suggestion of Tilling and others (1987) that their Sr determinations were suspect. By contrast, the Ba data are coherent for all three available data sets. The Rb data of the present study (fig. 5c), though in good agreement with each other, are somewhat higher than the Gunn (1971) data, as indicated in table 1.

Figure 7d (Sc, La and Hf) show that the INAA data for these incompatible, high-field-strength elements from Tilling and others (1987) are in good agreement with the INAA data of the present study. For similar elements not plotted here, the other rare-earth elements follow La, and the U levels also compare reasonably well, as indicated in table 1. By contrast, the Y data (fig. 7e) are noisy, and no two studies fall at the same concentration level, though the Gunn (1971) data seem to define the most coherent olivine-control line.

To summarize, most of the available trace-element data for samples from the 1959 eruption fall on linear arrays consistent with olivine control, even for elements where the different studies have obtained different concentration levels. Given that the samples consist of glass ± olivine ± chromite, the few data sets (some Zn and Y data) that do not define linear arrays must be regarded as of lower quality than those that do.

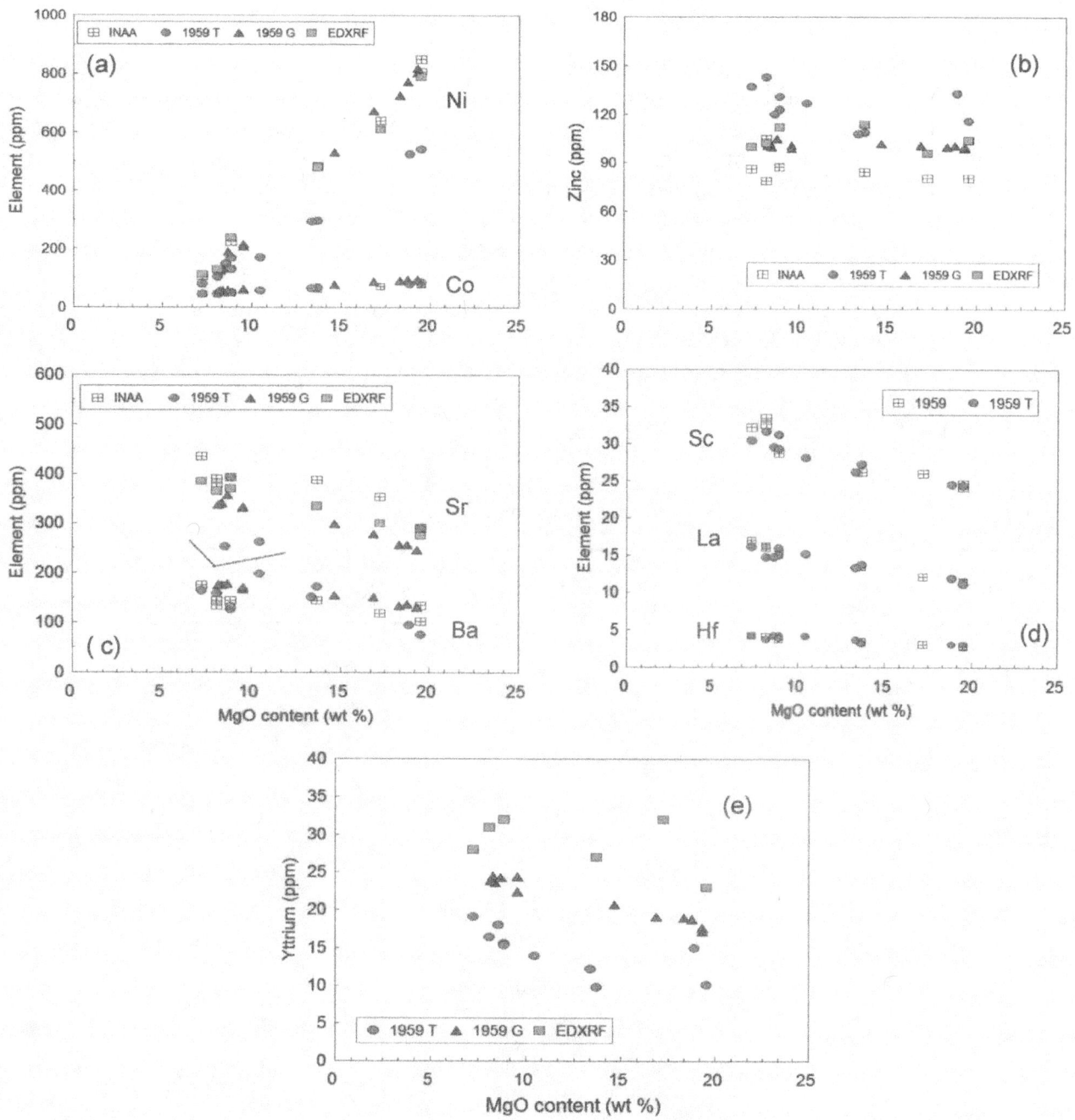

Figure 7.   Concentrations of nine elements, in parts per million (ppm), plotted against MgO content, in weight percent (wt %), for samples from the 1959 eruption. Up to four different data sets are available, as indicated in the key within each plot.

Overview of Processes Active in Kilauea Iki Lava Lake

Of the 84 samples included in this study, 78 are samples of drill core from Kilauea Iki lava lake, recovered from 1967 to 1988. Most are olivine-phyric basalt, but a few segregation veins and other internal differentiates and borehole oozes have been included to help flesh out the behavior of trace elements over the lower part of the line of descent of the fractionating liquid. In contrast to the eruption samples, which differ primarily in their olivine content, samples from the lava lake have been affected by lower-temperature processes where augite and plagioclase were also present as crystallizing phases.

Table 2 summarizes the processes that have affected Kilauea Iki samples, as described in Helz (1987a, 2009). The olivine content of the olivine-phyric samples varies greatly, with bulk MgO content in this suite ranging from 6.74 to over 25 percent. More of the lake has been affected by this process than any other, as indicated in table 2. The second most significant process is the upward migration of the low-density liquid present at the beginning of crystallization of plagioclase as described in Helz and others (1989). Most of the 78 lava lake samples have been affected by one or both of these processes, which took place in the molten core of the lake.

Table 2. Differentiation processes in Kilauea Iki lava lake, modified from Helz (1987a, 2009).
[+, plus; >, greater than; <, less than]

Stage of crystallization	Differentiation process	Depth range affected (meters)	Temperature range (ºC)
Processes occurring in molten core of lake, before formation of coherent crystal mush	Olivine settling	10 to 97+	>1180
	Lateral convection	20 to 43	1165–1170
	Diapiric melt transfer of minimum-density melt	13 to 94	1150–1160
Processes occurring within coherent crystal mush zones	Formation of ferrodiabasic segregation veins (coarse grained, sill-like, internal differentiates)	18 to 56	1100–1135
	Formation of vertical olivine-rich bodies (diapir tracks) that carried segregation vein melts through the mush zone at the base of the upper crust	18 to 58	<1140
	Formation of melt chimneys and speckled-rock plumes that carried differentiated melts upward from the lower mush zone atop the lower crust	78 to 95	<1140
Process occurring in rigid but partially molten rock	Flow of late-stage melts into fractures and open boreholes	Possible anywhere inside chilled margins	<1070

Lower-temperature processes include the formation of diabasic segregation veins and of the vertical structures that mark the passage of the ferrodiabasic liquid from the lower part of the lake to the upper parts. These processes, which occur within coherent crystal mush zones (table 2), leave conspicuous textural traces in the drill core. The suite of samples analyzed here includes four ferrodiabasic segregation veins and three oozes of similar composition, plus four samples of rocks having anomalous textures and compositions (two vertical olivine-rich bodies or "vorbs", one olivine-glass body, and one speckled-rock body) that mark them as having been zones of transport for the segregation-vein liquids.

The final process in table 2, which has produced the most extreme differentiates found in Kilauea Iki, is the flow of late-stage melts into naturally occurring fractures in the lake or, occasionally, into open boreholes. Table 3 presents bulk compositional data for all samples more fractionated than the ferrodiabasic segregation veins, for which data are included in this report.

The table includes three samples with MgO = 2.37–2.60 percent, two of which formed from melt found within segregation veins that had half-crystallized. One of these (KI67-2-85.7) flowed from a partially molten segregation into an open borehole and was recovered during redrilling. The other (KI81-2-88.6) is a naturally occurring internal differentiate of a segregation vein, of similar composition. The third extremely differentiated sample is KI79-5-163.0, shown in column 1 of table 3. This small vein formed when liquid flowed not from a partly crystallized segregation vein but from within olivine-rich matrix when the matrix fractured somewhat above its solidus.

This vein was too small to submit for major-element as well as trace-element analysis, so some of the powder was fused in a nitrogen atmosphere at extremely high temperature using the procedure of Jezek and others (1979), and the resulting glass was analyzed by microprobe. This same technique was applied to powder of sample KI81-2-88.6. Comparison of the analyses in columns 2 and 3 of table 3 shows that microprobe analysis of the fused glasses produces a reasonably accurate bulk composition for KI81-2-88.6, which suggests that the analysis in column 1 fairly represents the composition of sample KI79-5-163.0. If one compares this bulk composition with the various liquid lines of descent shown in Helz (1987a), the Al_2O_3, total iron as FeO, and CaO contents of KI79-5-163.0 are consistent with its having been interstitial liquid in an olivine-rich matrix, like the melts from KI81-1. By contrast, the other two extreme differentiates have compositions that mark them as derived from an olivine-poor source, like liquids from KI67-3, consistent with their occurrence as internal differentiates of segregation veins.

The final two columns in table 3 show bulk compositions of two melt-rich layers from the ooze that rose in borehole KI79-1, recovered as core KI79-1R (see descriptive log in Helz, 1993). This ooze underwent flow differentiation as it moved up, liberating an intermediate-stage liquid (MgO = 3.42–3.48 percent) that does not otherwise occur as a separate body in Kilauea Iki. These compositions are consistent with interstitial melts from intermediate olivine contents, like those from KI75-1 (Helz, 1987a).

Table 3. Major-element compositions of extreme differentiates from Kilauea Iki for which trace-element data have been obtained. The whole-rock gravimetric analyses are from Helz and others (1994), although here all iron is reported as FeO to facilitate comparison with the microprobe analyses.
[--, no data; <, less than]

Sample no.	1 KI79-5-163.0 small vein	2 KI81-2-88.6 vein in segregation vein	3 KI81-2-88.6 vein in segregation vein	4 KI67-2-85.7 ooze from segregation vein	5 KI79-1R1-167.8 melt layer in ooze	6 KI79-1R1-170.9 melt layer in ooze
Type of analysis	Fused glass microprobe	Fused glass microprobe	Gravimetric	Gravimetric	Gravimetric	Gravimetric
SiO_2	60.11	56.56	57.07	56.21	54.78	54.59
Al_2O_3	14.18	12.86	12.86	12.88	13.22	13.01
FeO (total)	7.59	11.70	11.61	12.03	11.63	11.97
MgO	2.57	2.50	2.37	2.60	3.42	3.48
CaO	4.51	6.11	6.08	6.33	7.08	7.07
Na_2O	4.25	3.50	3.55	3.53	3.41	3.37
K_2O	2.59	2.02	1.90	1.99	1.52	1.51
$H_2O\pm$	---	---	0.18	0.32	0.26	0.21
TiO_2	2.16	2.56	2.59	2.72	3.24	3.21
P_2O_5	0.66	0.84	0.96	0.88	0.74	0.69
MnO	0.08	0.14	0.18	0.20	0.18	0.19
Cr_2O_3	<0.01	<0.01	<0.01	0.00	<0.01	<0.01
Total	98.70	98.79	99.35	99.69	99.48	99.30

14

Trace-Element Variations in Kilauea Iki Lava Lake

Chemical variations in Kilauea Iki are most effectively presented on magnesia variation diagrams because of the large range of values for MgO. Such plots of the major elements show clearly the dominance of olivine control but also allow one to recognize the incoming of augite, plagioclase, and the Fe-Ti oxides (Helz and others, 1994). The following section discusses the variation of 16 trace elements versus MgO, selected to include all variation patterns observed. Elements omitted include the rare-earth elements (REE), whose chondrite-normalized patterns are discussed in a separate section below, and elements that were below the level of detection in many samples. The principal conclusions of this report are that there are few surprises in the trace-element data and that variations in the data are consistent with processes already inferred from major-element variations documented in earlier studies (Helz, 1987a; Helz and others, 1989; Helz, 2009).

Trace Elements Compatible with Olivine and (or) Chromite

The variations of Cr, Ni, and Zn as a function of MgO content are shown in figures 8a–c, with Cu versus MgO shown for comparison in figure 8d. Of these, Ni (like Co, which is not shown separately here) shows the simplest pattern, decreasing steadily as MgO, and hence the olivine content of the samples, decreases. There is no divergence between the 1959 eruption samples and cores drilled in various years.

Cr displays a similar overall decrease because most Cr is in chromite, and chromite occurs primarily as inclusions in olivine. However, a small group of very magnesian samples (outlined in fig. 8a) have relatively low Cr contents. These analyses (of samples 79-3-145.1, 81-1-169.9, 81-1-200.4, and 88-1-268.5) are all of structures related to the formation of segregation veins, as noted in the analytical tables. They are enriched in interstitial melt and depleted in augite relative to normal matrix rock with similar bulk MgO contents, hence their relatively low Cr levels. Finally, it should be noted that Cr shows a sudden drop to nearly zero for samples with MgO < 6.5 percent (the segregation veins and more extreme differentiates), presumably because they contain little olivine and no chromite. The more gradual decrease seen for Ni in the less magnesian samples may reflect the presence of some Ni in pyroxenes.

Figure 8c shows the EDXRF data for Zn, as they are more coherent than the INAA data and are consistent with Gunn's (1971) data. In the eruption samples, Zn increases very slightly as MgO content decreases, suggesting that Zn is only slightly fractionated between forsteritic olivine (average composition Fo_{86-87}) phenocrysts and the melt, as noted earlier by Gunn (1971). However, in core from Kilauea Iki, Zn clearly decreases throughout the olivine-control range (MgO = 6.5-27.5 percent). In this range, Zn is partitioned into the Fe-enriched olivine produced by re-equilibration of the original forsteritic olivine. Table 4 shows data confirming the uptake of Zn by olivine of Fo_{80-71}. The three samples highlighted in figure 8c, which run higher in Zn than most, are also enriched in Fe-rich olivine relative to other samples with similar MgO contents. Below 6.5 percent MgO, Zn increases significantly (peaking at 150 parts per million), then drops in the most extreme differentiates. The increase presumably reflects the paucity of olivine in the fractionating assemblage in the range of 3.5 to 6.5 percent MgO. The subsequent decline in Zn is presumably caused by partitioning of Zn into one or more of the Fe-Ti oxide minerals that begin to crystallize at ~4.5–5.5 percent MgO (Helz, 1987a; Helz and others, 1994).

15

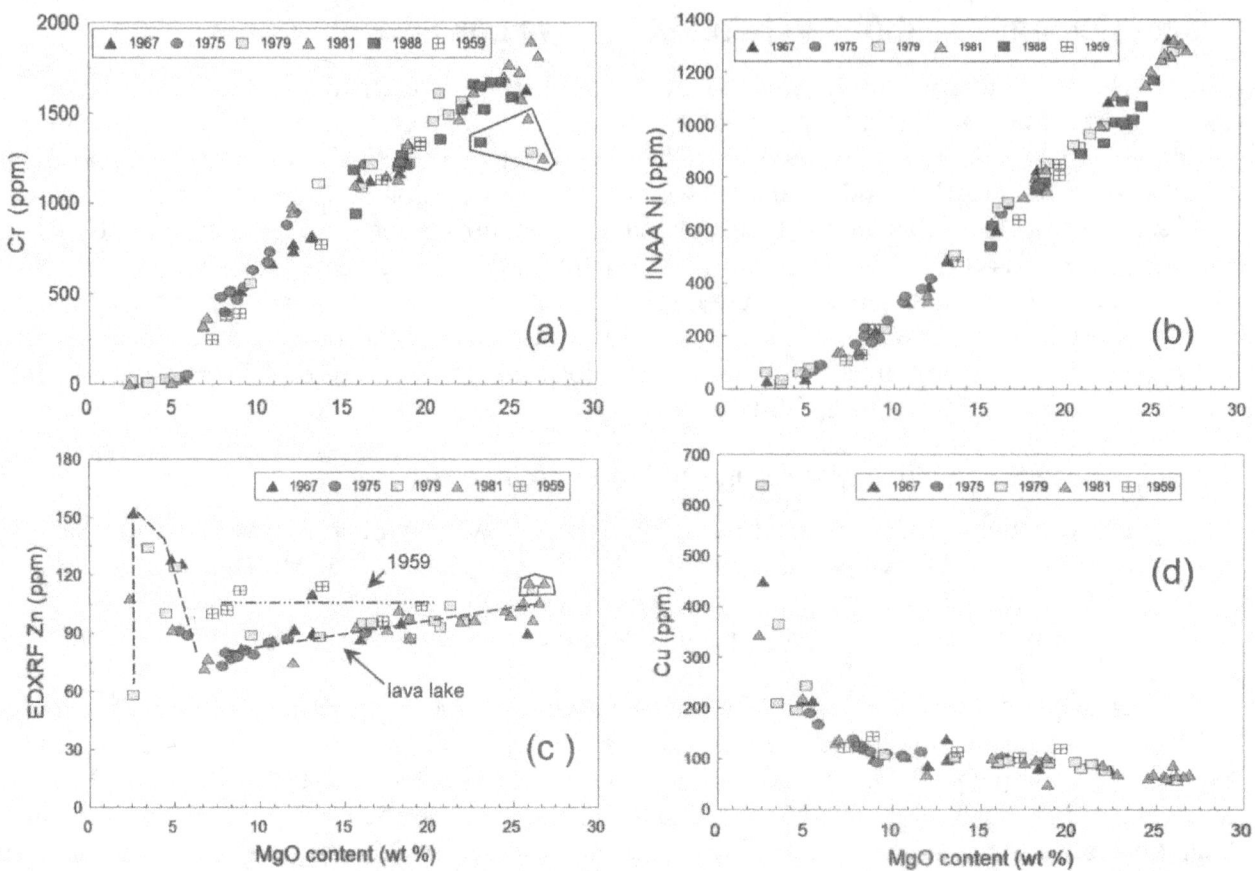

Figure 8. Cr, Ni, Zn, and Cu concentrations, in parts per million (ppm), versus MgO content, in weight percent (wt %), for drill core plus samples from the 1959 eruption, as indicated in the key within each plot. Fields in figures 8a and 8c enclose melt-enriched samples from structures associated with the formation of segregation veins. Lines in figure 8c show Zn compositional trends, as discussed in the text.

Table 4. Average olivine compositions in selected samples from Kilauea Iki lava lake.
[Quantities in weight percent unless otherwise noted. °C, degrees Celsius; ppm, parts per million; mol %, mol percent]

Sample no.	KI67-3-83.8	KI75-1-144.9	KI79-3-166.1	KI79-1-187.4
Temperature on quench (°C)	1076	1117	1071	1130
No. points	14	9	11	12
SiO_2	37.90	39.10	38.76	39.14
TiO_2	0.03	0.02	0.03	0.02
Al_2O_3	0.01	0.03	0.02	0.02
Cr_2O_3	0.01	0.02	0.02	0.03
FeO	25.59	19.82	21.35	18.51
NiO	0.20	0.26	0.26	0.27
MnO	0.34	0.28	0.30	0.27
MgO	36.19	41.12	39.86	41.78
CaO	0.28	0.28	0.26	0.29
Total	100.57	100.94	100.88	100.33
Zn (ppm)	154	121	140	96
Fo (mol %)	71.4	78.5	76.8	79.9

This complex behavior for Zn contrasts strongly with that of Cu (figure 8d), which is included here for comparison and exhibits the pattern of an incompatible trace element. Copper is chalcophile, of course, but the melt becomes saturated with immiscible sulfide liquid at so late a stage that sulfide is not a fractionating phase. The sample with the highest Cu content is the small vein KI79-5-163.0 (col. 1, table 3), which contains a number of blebs of pure chalcocite (Cu_2S), as documented in Pitcher and others (2009).

Trace Elements Compatible with Pyroxene and (or) Plagioclase

Only two elements in the suite investigated (Sc and Sr, in figs. 9a and 9b) show discernible effects of crystallization and fractionation of augite or plagioclase in magnesia variation diagrams. The first of these (Sc) peaks at roughly 7 to 8 percent MgO. As augite begins to crystallize (at MgO = 7.5 to 7.6 percent, Helz and Thornber, 1987), trivalent Sc is partitioned strongly into this new phase. Sc levels decrease sharply as augite crystallization proceeds, as can be seen in the Sc levels in samples with less than 5 percent MgO, in which the dominant pyroxene is pigeonite.

The EDXRF data for Sr (fig. 9b) are shown rather than the INAA data for Sr because they are much more coherent, though lacking data for the 1988 drill core. Strontium levels peak at MgO = 6–7 percent, where plagioclase begins to crystallize. Strontium then decreases slightly but not as drastically as Sc. This is because (1) it is not as strongly partitioned into plagioclase as Sc is into augite and (2) the most differentiated samples analyzed are still crystallizing abundant plagioclase, whereas augite crystallization is nearly complete.

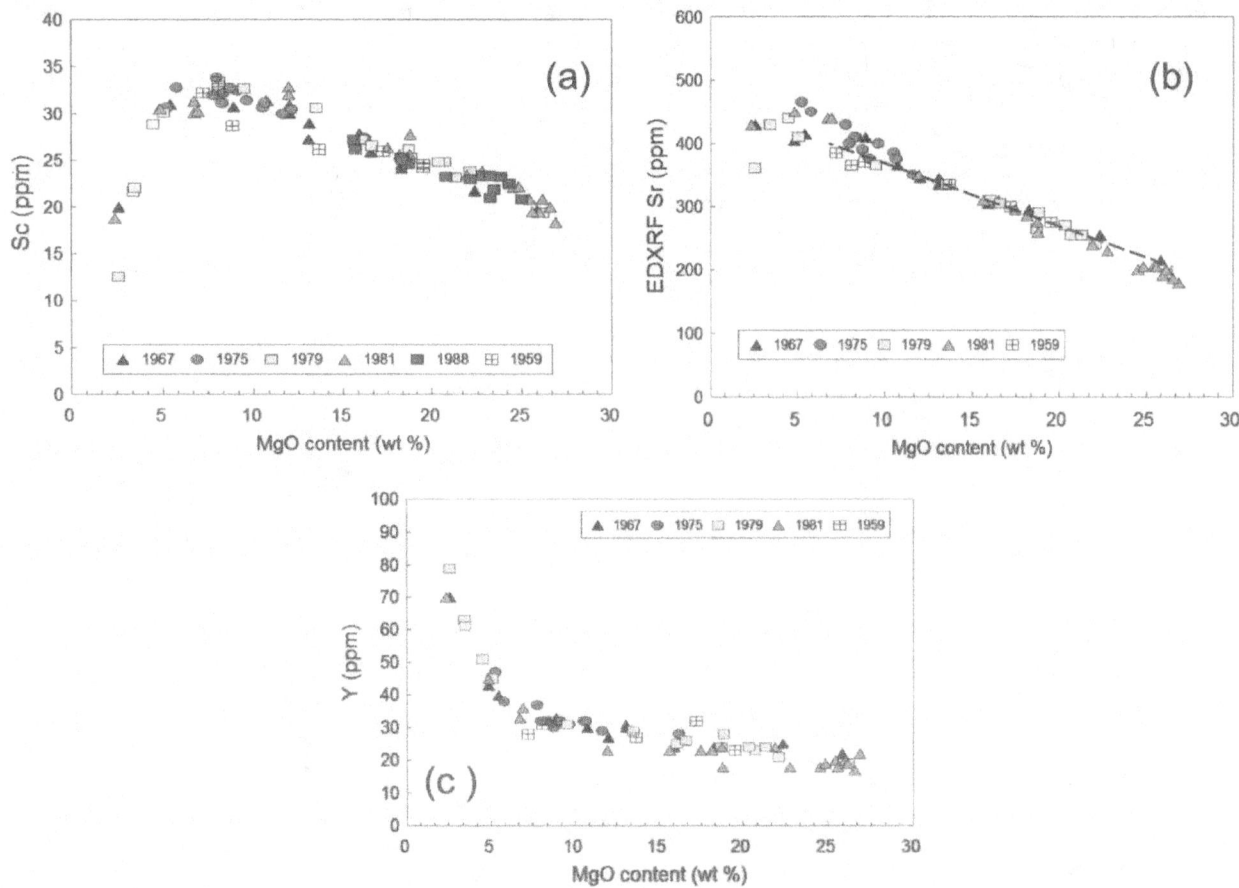

Figure 9. Sc, Sr, and Y concentrations, in parts per million (ppm), versus MgO content, in weight percent (wt %), for drill core samples plus samples from the 1959 eruption, as indicated in the key within each plot. Dashed line in figure 9b indicates olivine-control line, based on the 1959 eruption samples plus sample KI67-3-6.8, as discussed in the text.

The dashed line in figure 9b fits the 1959 eruption samples plus KI67-3-6.8, a very olivine-rich sample recovered at a depth of 6.8 feet in 1967, from the upper chill zone of the lava lake. These samples define a strict Fo_{86-87} olivine control line, so that their variation shows how Sr varies in samples affected only by olivine control. Note that the slope of this line is shallower than the overall array of samples from the lava lake. This is a recurring feature of the trace-element data, as it was for the relatively incompatible major elements (TiO_2, Na_2O, K_2O, P_2O_5, as discussed in Helz and Taggart, 2010). This rotation in trends is consistent with the migration of differentiated liquid upward in the lake (Helz, 1987a; Helz and others, 1989), as summarized in table 2. That line is not shown in figure 9a because the eruption samples are quite variable in their Sc levels, perhaps reflecting the two different components of this mixed-magma eruption (Wright, 1973; Helz, 1987b).

Figure 9c shows the variation of yttrium with MgO for all available data, for comparison with Sc. In spite of the incoherence of the various Y determinations for the 1959 eruption samples (fig. 7e), the overall pattern for Y in the lava lake is reasonably coherent, presumably because the range of concentrations of both Y and MgO are larger in figure 9c than those in figure 7e. The pattern, as expected, is that of a relatively incompatible trace element.

Incompatible Alkali and Alkaline Earth Trace Elements

Figure 10 shows how Rb, Ba, and Cs vary as a function of MgO content in the Kilauea Iki samples. The INAA data for Rb are shown because (1) there are INAA analyses of the 1988 drill core and (2) the two methods produced data sets of similar coherence. Both Rb and Ba are excluded from all fractionating phases in the lava lake, so they are strongly enriched in the most differentiated samples. The dashed lines in figures 10a and 10b are olivine control lines determined as in figure 9b. There is some divergence between the line and the array of lava lake samples for Ba, but very little for Rb.

The available Cs data are shown in figure 10c. There is a scattering of Cs values reported in tables A2–A6; in addition, table A1 contains Cs determinations made by recounting one group of samples months later (job CE92), as described above. The recount data fall on a plausible olivine-control line, suggesting that this later counting produces more reliable Cs numbers than the standard procedure.

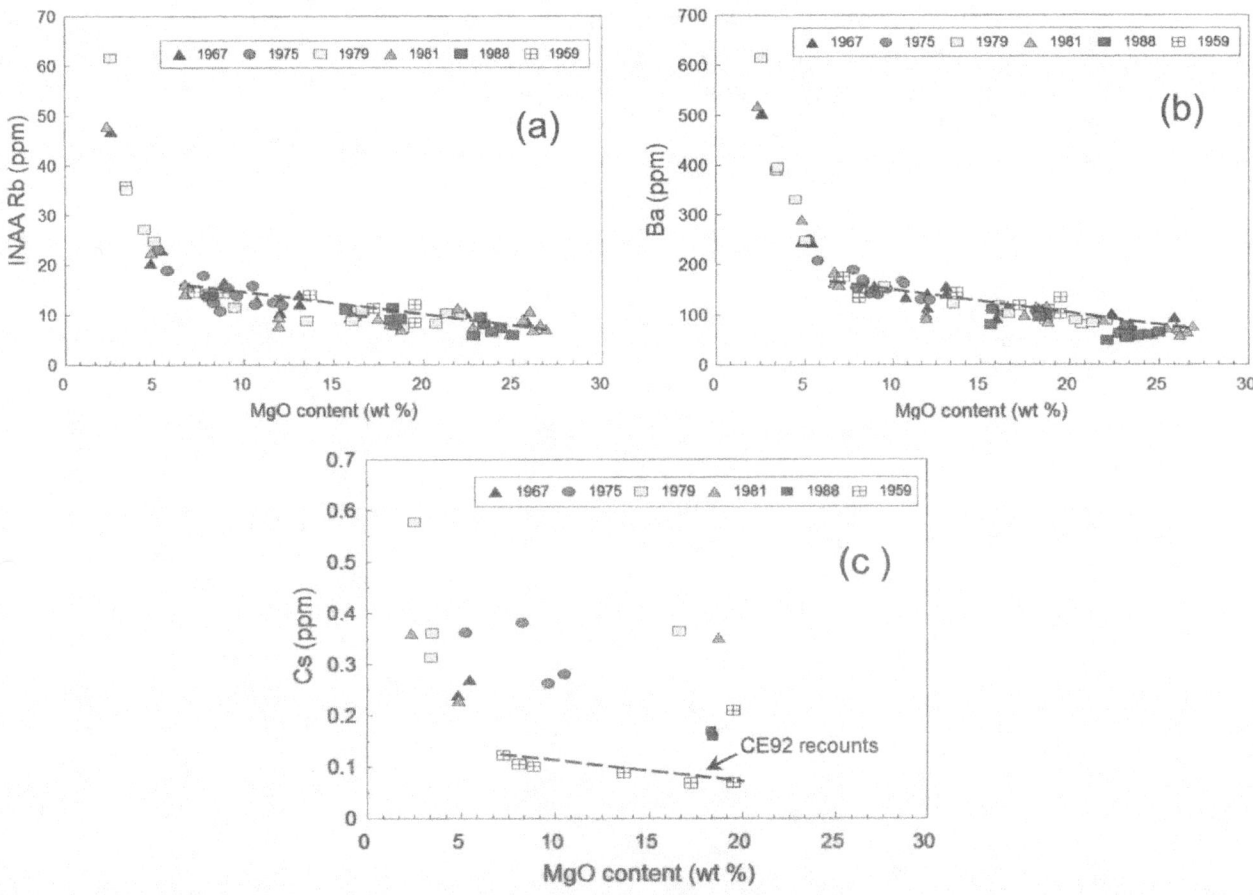

Figure 10.   Rb, Ba, and Cs concentrations, in parts per million (ppm), versus MgO content, in weight percent (wt %), for drill core samples plus samples from the 1959 eruption, as indicated by the key within each plot. Dashed lines in figures 10a and 10b are olivine-control lines, as discussed in the text. Figure 10c shows Cs for the few samples where Cs was reported.

High Field Strength Trace Elements

Figures 11a–f show magnesia variation diagrams for some high field strength elements (HFSE) other than the rare earths. Their patterns are all very similar in spite of large differences in concentration range among these elements. For the more tightly coherent elements (Zr, Hf, Ta, Th), the olivine-control line determined from the eruption samples plus KI67-3-6.8 is shown. The line is omitted for Nb and U because the reported values for the 1959 samples are more dispersed.

The array of data from the lava lake shows a consistent steeper slope than the strict olivine-control line, consistent again with extensive upward migration of differentiated liquid in the lake, as summarized in table 2. A unique feature of this group of trace elements is that a small group of samples from deep in the lava lake is depleted in these HFSE relative to most of the array. These samples include 81-1-270, 81-1-273.6 and 88-2-301.7 from zone VI (as noted in the analytical tables) and 88-2-322.2 (from zone VII). This extra level of depletion, seen also in K_2O and P_2O_5 levels, was attributed (Helz and Taggart, 2010) to these samples having lost more segregation-vein liquid than most other samples from similar depths. This second type of liquid extraction (table 2) involves a lower-temperature, more differentiated liquid than the migration of minimum-density melt. The higher-temperature process operated more uniformly on sections of the lake affected, as discussed in Helz and others (1989). By contrast, the lower-temperature segregation-liquid extraction is more local and more variable in its effects.

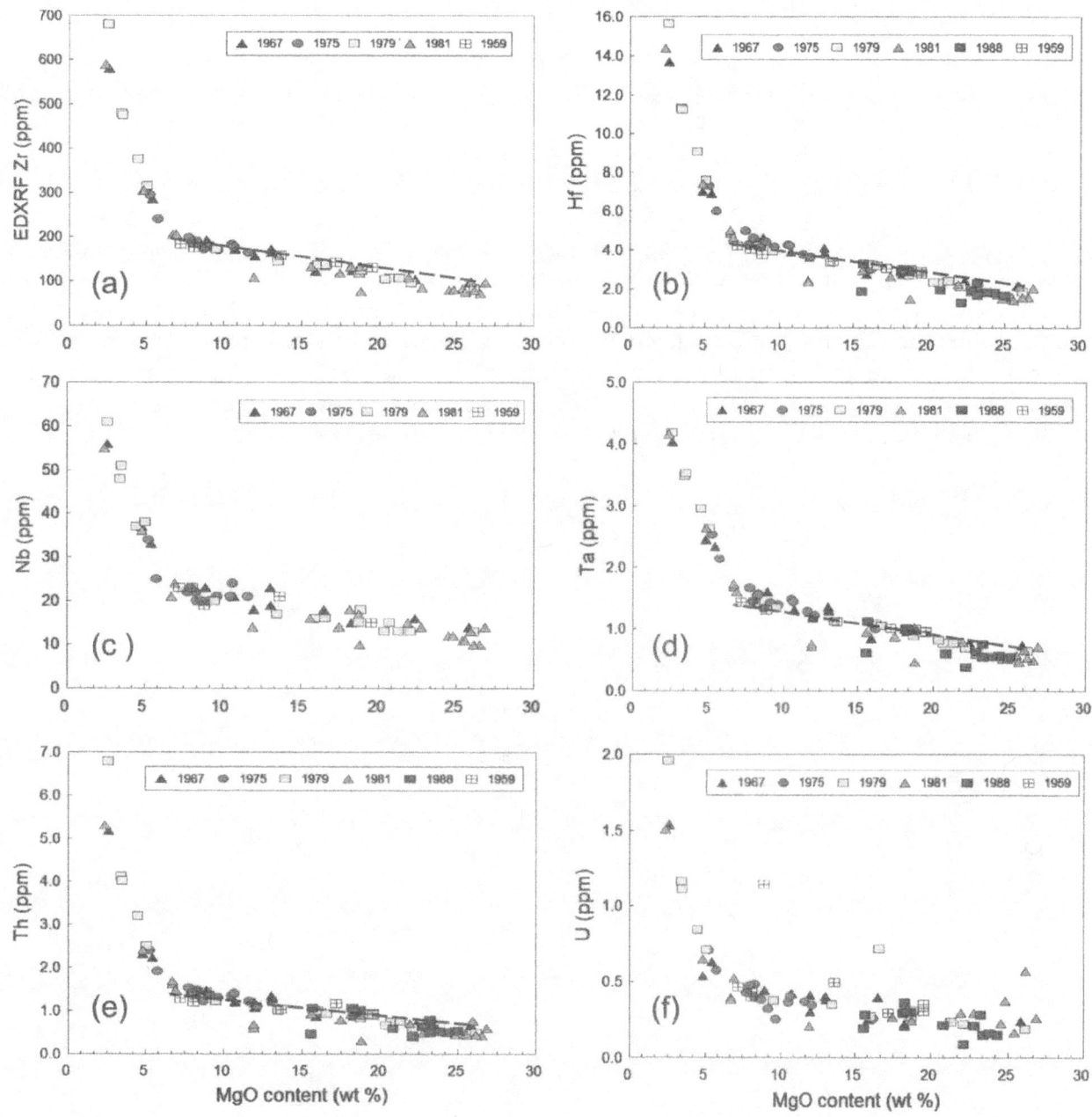

Figure 11. Trace elements, in parts per million (ppm), versus MgO contents, in weight percent (wt %), for drill core plus samples from the 1959 eruption, as indicated in the key within each plot. Dashed olivine-control lines, as in figure 9b, are discussed in the text.

Chondrite-Normalized Rare-Earth Element Patterns

Variations in rare-earth elements (REE) are usually displayed in diagrams where the concentrations of the REE in the various samples have been divided by the REE concentrations in chondrites. Figures 12 and 13 present REE patterns for selected samples from the present study, normalized using the REE concentrations reported in Anders and Ebihara (1982).

Figure 12 shows REE patterns for the 1959 eruption samples (table A1) plus that for sample 67-3-6.8 (table A2). This group of samples is used to define the olivine-control lines shown in several previous figures. Most patterns show a smooth decline in REE from La to Lu, with the patterns being slightly convex upward in the middle and declining steadily in the heavy REE. This pattern appears to be typical for Kilauea basalts (see, for example, Leeman and others, 1980), although it should be noted that this reference and most other collections of trace-element data for Kilauea lavas include a disproportionate number of samples from the 1959 eruption itself. REE concentration levels are inversely proportional to the olivine content of the samples, with sample 67-3-6.8 (MgO = 25.83 percent) being lowest and Iki-1 (MgO = 7.23 percent) being highest in REE.

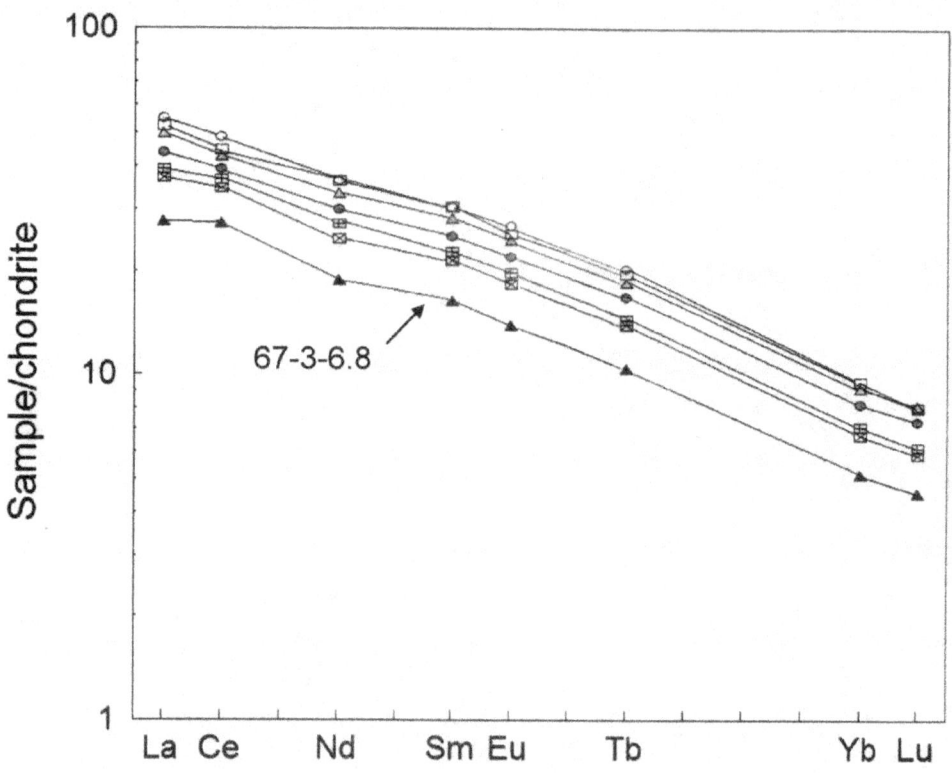

Figure 12.   Chondrite-normalized rare-earth element (REE) patterns for samples from the 1959 eruption plus shallow sample 67-3-6.8.

Figure 13 includes data for two groups of extreme samples from Kilauea Iki lava lake in order to show the effects of internal differentiation on the REE patterns. The upper group of samples (those with La = 80–115 times chondrite) include all segregation veins and equivalent glasses (five samples) plus the five more extreme differentiates shown in table 3. These samples again show that, in general, REE levels increase as MgO content decreases, although the single most REE-enriched sample is 79-5-163.0, which has slightly more MgO than the internal differentiates from segregation veins (table 3).

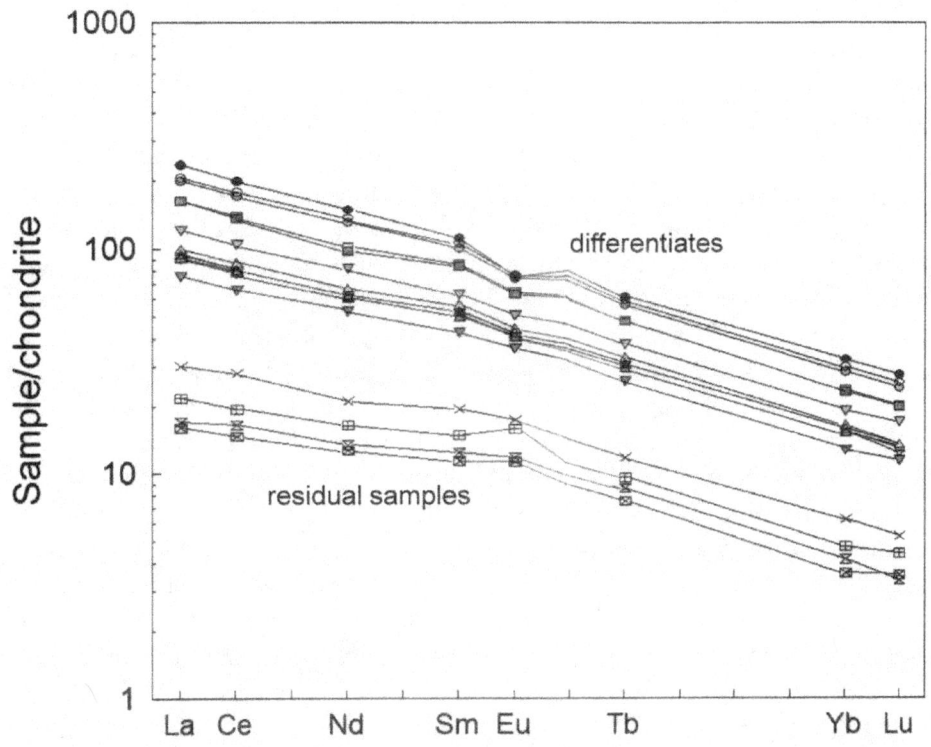

Figure 13. Chondrite-normalized rare-earth element (REE) patterns for segregation veins and glasses (five triangles), differentiated oozes from KI79-1R (two rectangles) and small late veins and oozes (three ovals), together with four strongly depleted samples from zones VI and VII.

The segregation-vein patterns have barely perceptible negative Eu anomalies, but the five more differentiated samples are clearly depleted in Eu relative to adjacent REE. Such negative Eu anomalies occur because the fraction of Eu present as Eu^{+2} is fractionated by plagioclase. The ratio of divalent to trivalent Eu varies inversely with oxygen fugacity, so that Eu anomalies are more easily generated at low oxygen fugacity (Drake, 1975; Drake and Weill, 1975). Oxidation conditions in Kilauea Iki lava lake vary from fayalite-magnetite-quartz (FMQ) to nickel-nickel oxide (NNO), based on compositions of coexisting ilmenite and magnetite (Buddington and Lindsley, 1964), so Eu anomalies are not conspicuous. They are discernible in the segregation veins but are best developed in the extreme differentiates, which correspond to melts present after extensive crystallization of plagioclase.

Figure 13 also includes REE patterns for the four especially depleted samples (81-1-270, 81-1-273.6, 88-2-301.7, and 88-2-322.2) that were singled out in figure 11. All four have positive Eu anomalies, with that in the least depleted (81-1-273.6) sample having the smallest. Evidently this material is complementary to the segregation veins and other differentiates, supporting the idea that some of the liquid in the segregation veins originated in zones VI and VII, as proposed in Helz and Taggart (2010).

Discussion and Summary

The purpose of obtaining trace-element data on a subset of samples from Kilauea Iki lava lake was to document their behavior in a basaltic system undergoing extensive fractionation at low pressure and water activity. Earlier studies suggested that open system behavior in Kilauea Iki lava lake has been very limited. Some volatiles (CO_2, some chlorine, and much of the original H_2O present in the lava) were lost during the eruption or very shortly thereafter, although in the same report Helz and others (1994) showed that there was no loss of either F or Cl from subsequent lake samples, at least from 1967 through 1981. Sulfur was lost gradually over time, with the melt degassing significant sulfur during the 1967–1976 drilling episodes, as documented in Helz and Wright (1983). One other element lost during the aging and crystallization of the lava lake is Re, as documented by Pitcher and others (2009).

The overall pattern of enrichment or depletion of individual trace elements is summarized in figure 14. In this figure, the trace-element concentrations for the three most differentiated samples analyzed from the lava lake have been normalized to the average of the following four samples: 79-3-160.5 (zone IV, MgO = 16.05 percent), 79-3-172.8 (zone IV, MgO = 18.71 percent), 79-5-260.0 (lower chill, MgO = 18.84 percent), and 79-5-300.5 (lower chill, MgO = 16.61 percent). All four samples are undifferentiated with respect to eruption samples and lie very close to the olivine-control lines shown in figures 9–11 but were not used to define those lines. Their average MgO content is 17.71 percent, somewhat higher than the average for the lava lake, which was estimated by Wright (1973) as 15.5 percent MgO. This denominator was used because there are no samples that have the lake's average MgO content among those analyzed for trace elements. Figure 14 also includes enrichment factors for K and P, for purposes of comparison with the enrichment factors for the various trace elements.

For elements shown in figure 8 plus Co, the enrichment factors rise steeply from left to right, being lowest for Cr (concentrated in chromite) and highest for Cu (concentrated in late-separating sulfide). The figure shows that Co lies between Ni and Zn in its compatibility with olivine, consistent with other studies (for example, Gunn, 1971). The next group of elements (from fig. 9) includes the few which, along with Zn, are mildly compatible with some of the major phases (augite, plagioclase) crystallizing in the lava lake. Note that Y, the most incompatible in this group, is distinctly less enriched than the other incompatible elements.

The remaining two groups of elements are all highly incompatible, with enrichment factors of 3.4 to 7.4. They are no more highly concentrated than K and P, however, so no special processes of trace-element enrichment were active in the lava lake. In particular, there is no evidence for the "volatile transfer" process invoked by Richter and Moore (1966) to explain some erroneous analyses from the earliest (1960–1961) drill core. It should be noted that apatite has begun to crystallize in sample 79-5-163.0; this crystallization has affected its P enrichment factor and may have affected the concentrations of the HFSE (other than Th and U) in this sample as well.

The results presented in this report show that, for the elements considered here, the lava lake has indeed been a closed system and that the behavior of the trace elements is completely congruent with fractionation processes inferred on the basis of major-element compositional variations. These data, coupled with determination of trace elements on the glasses and individual crystalline phases, may allow determination of trace-element partitioning coefficients for the principal phases in basalt over a wide range of temperatures.

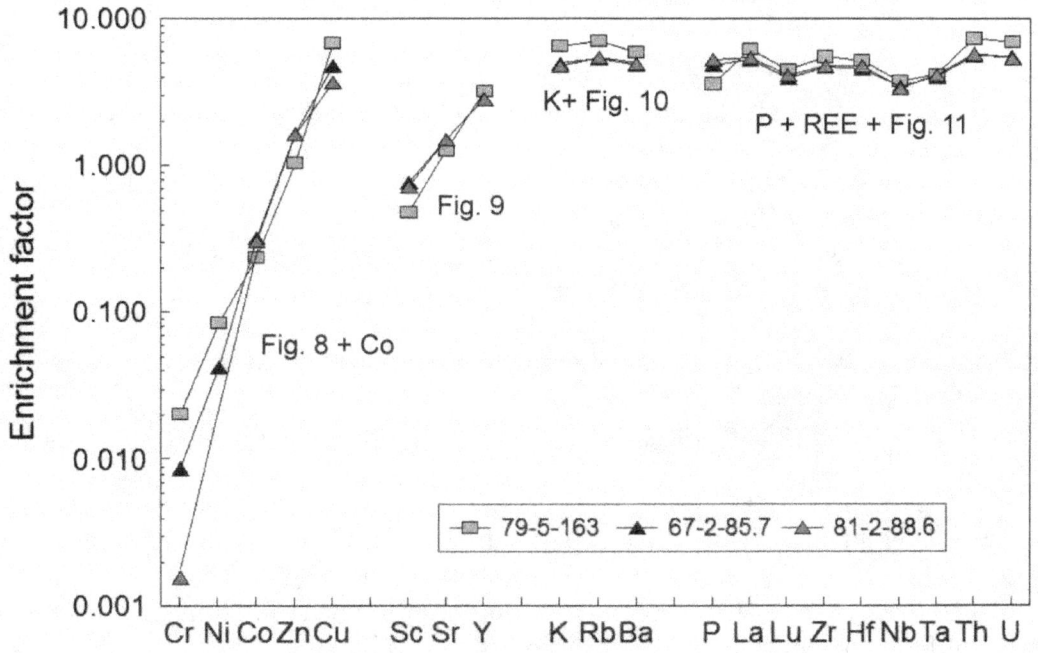

Figure 14. Enrichment factors for the three most differentiated samples from Kilauea Iki lava lake, compared with the average of four undifferentiated samples with MgO = 16.05 to 18.84 weight percent. Elements shown include those from figures 8–11, plus Co, K, and P, with the REE represented by La and Lu.

References Cited

Anders, E., and Ebihara, M., 1982, Solar-system abundances of the elements: Geochimica Cosmochimica Acta, v. 46, p. 2363–2380.

Aruscavage, P.J., and Crock, J.G., 1987, Atomic absorption methods: U.S. Geological Survey Bulletin 1770, p. C1–C6.

Baedecker, P.A., and Grossman, J.N., 1989, The computer analysis of high resolution gamma-ray spectra from instrumental activation analysis experiments: U.S. Geological Survey Open-File Report 89–454, 88 p.

Baedecker, P.A., and McKown, D.M., 1987, Instrumental neutron activation analysis of geochemical samples: U.S. Geological Survey Bulletin 1770, H1–H14.

Barth, G.A., Kleinrock, M.C., and Helz, R.T., 1994, The magma body at Kilauea Iki lava lake–Potential insights into mid-ocean ridge magma chambers: Journal of Geophysical Research, v. 99, p. 7199–7217.

Buddington, A.F., and Lindsley, D.H., 1964, Iron-titanium oxide minerals and synthetic equivalents: Journal of Petrology v. 5, p. 310–357.

Drake, M.J., 1975, The oxidation state of europium as an indicator of oxygen fugacity: Geochimica et Cosmochimica Acta, v. 39, p. 55–64.

Drake, M.J., and Weill, D.F., 1975, Partition of Sr, Ba, Ca, Y, Eu^{+2}, Eu^{+3}, and other REE between plagioclase feldspar and magmatic liquid—An experimental study: Geochimica et Cosmochimica Acta, v. 39, p. 689–712.

Grossman, J.N., and Baedecker, P.A., 1987, Interactive methods for data reduction and quality control in INAA: Journal of Radioanalytical and Nuclear Chemistry, v. 113, p. 43–59.

Gunn, B.M., 1971, Trace-element partition during olivine fractionation of Hawaiian basalts: Chemical Geology, v. 8, p. 1–13.

Helz, R.T., 1980, Crystallization history of Kilauea Iki lava lake as seen in drill core recovered in 1967–1979: Bulletin Volcanologique, v. 43–4, p. 675–701.

Helz, R.T., 1987a, Differentiation behavior of Kilauea Iki lava lake, Kilauea Volcano, Hawaii—An overview of past and current work, in Mysen, B.O., ed., Magmatic Processes—Physicochemical Principles: Geochemical Society Special Publication 1, p. 241–258.

Helz, R.T., 1987b, Character of olivines in lavas of the 1959 eruption of Kilauea Volcano and its bearing on eruption dynamics, in Decker, R.W., Wright, T.L., and Stauffer, P.H., eds., Volcanism in Hawaii: U.S. Geological Survey Professional Paper 1350, p. 691–722.

Helz, R.T., 1993, Drilling report and core logs for the 1988 drilling of Kilauea Iki lava lake, Kilauea Volcano, Hawaii, with summary descriptions of the occurrence of foundered crust and fractures in the drill core: U.S. Geological Survey Open-File Report 93–15, 57 p.

Helz, R.T., 2009, Processes active in mafic magma chambers—The example of Kilauea Iki lava lake, Hawaii: Lithos, v. 111, p. 37–46.

Helz, R.T., and Taggart, J.E., Jr., 2010, Whole-rock analyses of core samples from the 1988 drilling of Kīlauea Iki lava lake, Hawaii: U.S. Geological Survey Open-File Report 2010–1093, 47 p.

Helz, R.T., and Thornber, C.R., 1987, Geothermometry of Kilauea Iki lava lake: Bulletin of Volcanology, v. 49, p. 651–668.

Helz, R.T., and Wright, T.L., 1983, Drilling report and core logs for the 1981 drilling of Kilauea Iki lava lake (Kilauea Volcano, Hawaii), with comparative notes on earlier (1967–1979) drilling experiences: U.S. Geological Survey Open-File Report 83–326, 66 p.

Helz, R.T., Banks, N.G., Casadevall, T.J., Fiske, R.S., and Moore, R.B., 1984, A catalogue of drill core recovered from Kilauea Iki lava lake from 1967 to 1979: U.S. Geological Survey Open-File Report 84–484, 72 p.

Helz, R.T., Kirschenbaum, H., and Marinenko, J.W., 1989, Diapiric transfer of melt in Kilauea Iki lava lake, Hawaii—A quick, efficient process of igneous differentiation: Geological Society of America Bulletin, v. 101, p. 578–594.

Helz, R.T., Kirschenbaum, H., Marinenko, J.W., and Qian, Rachel, 1994, Whole-rock analyses of core samples from the 1967, 1975, 1979 and 1981 drillings of Kilauea Iki lava lake, Hawaii: U.S. Geological Survey Open-File Report 94–684, 65 p.

Jezek, P.A., Sinton, J.M., Jarosewich, E., and Obermeyer, C.R., 1979, Fusion of rock and mineral poweders for electron microprobe analysis: Smithsonian Contributions to the Earth Sciences, v. 22, p. 46–53.

Johnson, R.G., and King, B.-S. L., 1987, Energy-dispersive X-ray fluorescence spectrometry: U.S. Geological Survey Bulletin 1770, p. F1–F5.

Kirschenbaum, Herbert, 1983, The classical chemical analysis of silicate rocks—The old and the new: U.S. Geological Survey Bulletin 1547, 55 p.

Leeman, W.P., Budahn, J.R., Gerlach, D.C., Smith, D.R., and Powell, B.N., 1980, Origin of Hawaiian tholeiites—Trace-element constraints: American Journal of Science, v. 280–A, p. 794–819.

Lichte, F.E., Golightly, D.W., and Lamothe, P.J., 1987, Inductively coupled plasma-atomic emission spectroscopy: U.S. Geological Survey Bulletin 1770, p. B1–10.

Murata, K.J., and Richter, D.H., 1966, Chemistry of the lavas of the 1959–60 eruption of Kilauea Volcano, Hawaii: U.S. Geological Survey Professional Paper 537–A, 26 p.

Pitcher, L., Helz, R.T., Walker, R.J., and Piccoli, P., 2009, Fractionation of the platinum-group elements and Re during crystallization of basalt in Kilauea Iki lava lake, Hawaii: Chemical Geology, v. 260, p. 196–210.

Richter, D.H., and Moore, J.G., 1966, Petrology of the Kilauea Iki lava lake, Hawaii: U.S. Geological Survey Professional Paper 537–B, 26 p.

Richter, D.H., and Murata, K.J., 1966, Petrography of the lavas of the 1959–60 eruption of Kilauea Volcano, Hawaii: U.S. Geological Survey Professional Paper 537–D, 12 p.

Tilling, R.I., Wright, T.L., and Millard, H.T., Jr., 1987, Trace-element chemistry of Kīlauea and Mauna Loa lava in space and time—A reconnaissance, in Decker, R.W., Wright, T.L., and Stauffer, P.H., eds., Volcanism in Hawaii: U.S. Geological Survey Professional Paper 1350, v. 1, p. 641–690.

Wright, T.L., 1971, Chemistry of Kilauea and Mauna Loa lava in space and time. U.S. Geological Survey Professional Paper 735, 40 p.

Wright, T.L., 1973, Magma mixing as illustrated by the 1959 eruption, Kilauea Volcano, Hawaii: Geological Society of America Bulletin, v. 84, p. 849–858.

Table A1. Instrumental neutron-activation analyses of trace elements for samples from the 1959 Kilauea Iki eruption.

[Most whole-rock major-element analyses (S-numbers) are in Murata and Richter (1966). Iki-3 analysis is in Helz and Taggart (2010). Mixing fractions are from Wright (1973). wt %, weight percent; ppm, parts per million; nd, not determined; °C, degrees Celsius; <, less than]

Field no.	Iki-1	Iki-58	Iki-58R	Iki-22	Iki-22R	Iki-3	Iki-44	Iki-38
Lab. no.	S-2	S-1	S-1	S-5	S-5	D-571889	S-7	S-25
Job no.	CE92	CE92	CG74	CE92	CG74	CE92	CE92	CE92
MgO wt. %	7.23	8.08	8.08	19.52	19.52	17.2	13.67	8.85
Sc ppm	32.2	32.6	33.4	24.2	24.6	26.0	26.2	28.7
Cr ppm	246	378	385	1318	1342	1130	772	390
Co ppm	45.6	45.6	45.4	80.1	78.5	71.1	63.0	49.5
Ni ppm	107	130	131	808	850	640	483	225
Zn ppm	86	79	105	80.6	104	81	84	87
As ppm	<2	<0.7	<2	<0.6	<0.9	<0.6	1.19	4.40
Se ppm	nd	nd	nd	nd	nd	nd	nd	nd
Rb ppm	14.6	13.8	14.3	12.1	8.5	11.4	14.1	14.5
Sr ppm	440	390	380	291	290	354	390	390
Zr ppm	210	250	180	155	140	200	220	170
Mo ppm	<4	<5	<5	<5	<5	<5	<4	3.2
Sb ppm	<0.2	<0.09	<0.1	0.112	<0.1	<0.07	0.51	2.01
Cs ppm	0.123	0.106	<0.2	0.070	0.21	0.069	0.089	0.101
Ba ppm	175	133	144	134	102	118	145	144
La ppm	17.0	16.0	16.2	11.4	11.5	12.1	13.5	15.4
Ce ppm	39.1	35.5	36.4	27.7	27.8	29.5	31.6	34.6
Nd ppm	21.6	21.6	1.9	14.9	14.7	16.3	17.9	20.1
Sm ppm	5.93	5.75	6.17	4.09	4.27	4.40	4.89	5.53
Eu ppm	1.95	1.84	1.88	1.306	1.37	1.43	1.59	1.78
Tb ppm	0.95	0.94	0.90	0.66	0.644	0.68	0.78	0.87
Yb ppm	1.92	1.97	1.99	1.34	1.44	1.47	1.71	1.90
Lu ppm	0.255	0.265	0.248	0.198	0.176	0.196	0.233	0.259
Hf ppm	4.22	4.04	4.06	2.77	2.89	3.04	3.42	3.78
Ta ppm	1.44	1.44	1.41	0.96	0.95	1.02	1.12	1.31
Au ppb	<8	<5	<2	13	<2	<6	9.1	5.45
Th ppm	1.28	1.21	1.36	0.91	0.94	1.17	1.03	1.43
U ppm	0.46	0.43	0.40	0.31	0.35	0.29	0.49	1.14
Phase of eruption	1	1	1	1	1	1	1	17
Fraction S-1/(S-1+S-2)	0	1	1	0.68	0.68	0.75	0.057	0
Quenching temperature (°C)	1142	---1144---		---1217---		1213	1187	---

Table A2. Instrumental neutron-activation analyses of trace elements for samples from the 1967 Kilauea Iki drill core.

[Major-element analyses are in Helz and others (1994). wt %, weight percent; ppm, parts per million; nd, not determined; <, less than]

Field no.	67-1-89.0	67-2-17.0	67-2-17.0R	67-2-59.8	67-2-79.9	67-2-85.7	67-2-89.5	67-2-94.6
Lab. no.	D-102046	W-214299		W-214301	W-214302	D-102049	D-102048	D-103993
Job no.	CG74	CE76	CG74	CE76	CE76	CE76	CE76	CE76
MgO (wt %)	4.83	18.26	18.26	16.53	22.34	2.60	13.07	15.91
Sc ppm	30.5	24.6	24.2	25.9	21.7	20.0	27.3	27.9
Cr ppm	39.7	1238	1167	1125	1562	10.4	811	1128
Co ppm	39.6	80.5	76.3	72.5	94.0	24.9	68.3	71.7
Ni ppm	39	816	830	698	1090	32	491	602
Zn ppm	142	102.1	104	95	100	165	119	92
As ppm	<0.7	1.15	<0.9	1.6	<0.6	<1	<8	1.05
Se ppm	nd	<2	nd	<2	<0.9	<2	<2	<0. 8
Rb ppm	20.4	9.3	9.3	10.5	10.4	47.0	14.1	9.6
Sr ppm	399	391	315	440	<400	500	403	450
Zr ppm	272	165	130	145	102	550	123	<150
Mo ppm	<6	<6	<5	<4	<6	3.8	<4	<6
Sb ppm	<0.2	0.15	<0.09	<0.08	<0.07	0.28	<0.2	0.15
Cs ppm	0.24	<0.2	<0.1	<0.2	<0.2	<0.2	<0.2	<0.2
Ba ppm	246	111	101	117	101	503	156	93
La ppm	29.0	11.23	11.0	12.5	9.7	61.5	16.0	10.8
Ce ppm	65.7	27.0	27.0	30.3	24.6	137.5	37.1	26.1
Nd ppm	36.5	14.9	14.6	15.4	12.3	78.4	20.4	14.8
Sm ppm	10.38	4.21	4.17	4.71	3.61	19.6	5.86	4.16
Eu ppm	3.05	1.326	1.34	1.50	1.12	5.41	1.81	1.36
Tb ppm	1.46	0.648	0.637	0.70	0.54	2.63	0.895	0.68
Yb ppm	3.20	1.38	1.44	1.53	1.12	5.89	1.90	1.35
Lu ppm	0.415	0.186	0.184	0.204	0.165	0.769	0.242	0.188
Hf ppm	7.02	2.88	2.77	3.20	2.41	13.69	4.09	2.76
Ta ppm	2.45	0.973	0.96	1.07	0.775	4.04	1.35	0.85
Au ppb	<9	<6	<0.7	<6	<3	<7	<9	<1
Th ppm	2.32	0.92	0.88	0.96	0.69	5.19	1.35	0.88
U ppm	0.54	0.22	0.21	0.40	0.22	1.54	0.40	0.25
Type of sample	glass in bit	(I)	(I)	foundered crust	foundered crust	ooze	leopard rock	foundered crust
Contains glass?	yes	no	no	yes	yes	yes	yes	yes
Quenching temperature	high	low	low	medium	high	high	high	high

Table A2. Instrumental neutron-activation analyses of trace elements for samples from the 1967 Kilauea Iki drill core.—Continued

Field no.	67-3-6.8	67-3-27.5	67-3-27.5R	67-3-39.0	67-3-47.8	67-3-58.0	67-3-87.0
Lab. no.	W-214121	D-103976		D-103977	D-103978	D-103979	D-102054
Job no.	CD53	CE76	CG74	CD53	CD53	CE76	CG74
MgO wt %	25.83	12.01	12.01	10.73	13.10	8.91	5.44
Sc ppm	19.58	30.89	30.0	31.4	29.0	30.7	31.0
Cr ppm	1630	773	739	670	819	516	40.4
Co ppm	104.4	60.6	57.3	56.9	65.0	47.4	39.9
i ppm	1327	389	386	327	485	223	89
Zn ppm	96.4	103.7	103	106	109	107	140
As ppm	<0.9	1.4	<1	<1	<0.6	1.9	<0.8
Se ppm	<3	<2	nd	<3	<2	<2	nd
Rb ppm	8.5	10.5	13.3	12.0	12.2	16.5	23.0
Sr ppm	<400	418	366	406	370	448	420
Zr ppm	118	180	<130	200	153	180	230
Mo ppm	<6	<6	<6	<8	<5	<5	<5
Sb ppm	<0.09	<0.1	<0.1	0.19	<0.07	0.15	<0.2
Cs ppm	<0.2	<0.2	<0.3	<0.3	<0.2	<0.2	0.27
Ba ppm	94	142	114	138	141	156	244
La ppm	8.56	14.4	14.0	15.6	15.21	18.1	27.9
Ce ppm	22.1	34.0	33.5	36.8	36.3	41.4	62.8
Nd ppm	11.2	20.0	18.4	21.2	21.6	23.4	36.3
Sm ppm	3.20	5.41	5.41	5.83	5.69	6.58	10.0
Eu ppm	1.010	1.73	1.71	1.83	1.81	2.11	2.97
Tb ppm	0.489	0.802	0.79	0.876	0.84	0.99	1.41
Yb ppm	1.07	1.77	1.80	1.86	1.79	2.18	3.18
Lu ppm	0.145	0.235	0.218	0.256	0.253	0.292	0.393
Hf ppm	2.16	3.65	3.63	3.90	3.85	4.61	6.92
Ta ppm	0.739	1.22	1.18	1.31	1.30	1.61	2.34
Au ppb	<5	<9	<1	7.6	<5	<6	<4
Th ppm	0.67	1.07	1.19	1.21	1.28	1.47	2.23
U ppm	0.24	0.30	0.41	0.42	0.38	0.44	0.63
Type of sample	(I)	(I)	(I)	(I)	(II)	(II)	glass in bit
Contains glass?	no	no	no	no	no	yes	
Quenching temperature	low	low	low	low	medium	medium	high

Table A3. Instrumental neutron-activation analyses of trace elements for samples from the 1975 Kilauea Iki drill core.
[Major-element analyses are in Helz and others (1994). wt %, weight percent; ppm, parts per million; <, less than]

Field no.	75-1-60.9	75-1-75.2	75-1-85.5	75-1-95.0	75-1-110	75-1-114.9		75-1-121.5
Lab. no.	D-103844	D-103846	D-103848	D-103850	D-103852	D-103853		D-103855
						a	b	
Job no.	CD53	CD53	CD53	CE76	CE76	CE76	CE76	CD53
MgO wt %	10.52	5.77	8.33	9.64	8.27	5.26	5.26	7.77
Sc ppm	30.6	32.8	32.2	31.4	31.1	31.1	30.3	31.9
Cr ppm	674	50.1	515	630	504	20.2	19.9	479
Co ppm	53.3	40.9	45.5	50.7	44.9	42.7	42.1	43.6
Ni ppm	331	91	229	257	199	63	72	169
Zn ppm	103	126	107	102.9	106	137	133	109
As ppm	<0.8	<1	<0.6	<0.6	<0.9	<1	<1	<0.9
Se ppm	<2	<2	<3	<0.8	<2	<3	<3	<3
Rb ppm	15.8	18.8	12.4	13.8	13.9	23.0	23	17.9
Sr ppm	440	506	460	470	426	510	510	440
Zr ppm	157	229	196	117	190	290	310	174
Mo ppm	<5	3.1	<4	<5	<6	<4	2.8	<3
Sb ppm	0.149	<0.1	0.096	<0.2	<0.09	<0.1	0.17	<0.09
Cs ppm	0.281	<0.3	<0.2	0.26	0.380	0.36	<0.2	<0.2
Ba ppm	167	207	165	151	170	263	244	190
La ppm	16.7	23.3	17.7	15.8	17.9	28.3	28.1	19.0
Ce ppm	39.8	52.7	42.2	36.7	41.7	64.0	64.2	44.3
Nd ppm	23.2	31.6	24.2	22.4	23.4	37.7	36.5	26.4
Sm ppm	6.17	8.26	6.61	5.98	6.60	9.91	9.63	6.94
Eu ppm	1.92	2.63	2.07	1.89	2.07	3.05	2.95	2.21
Tb ppm	0.88	1.21	0.96	0.92	0.98	1.38	1.39	1.016
Yb ppm	2.00	2.63	2.16	2.07	2.22	3.20	3.15	2.22
Lu ppm	0.272	0.364	0.282	0.261	0.295	0.427	0.417	0.306
Hf ppm	4.27	6.00	4.57	4.15	4.64	7.33	7.27	4.97
Ta ppm	1.48	2.13	1.57	1.39	1.55	2.55	2.52	1.67
Au ppb	<5	<3	<3	<6	<2	<9	<6	<4
Th ppm	1.35	1.92	1.46	1.30	1.43	2.40	2.41	1.52
U ppm	0.36	0.58	0.39	0.25	0.48	0.71	<0.9	0.42
Type of sample	(II)	segregation vein	(II)	(II)	(II)	segregation vein		(II)
Contains glass?	no	no	no	no	no	---- no-----		no
Quenching temperature	low	low	low	low	medium	medium		medium

Table A3. Instrumental neutron-activation analyses of trace elements for samples from the 1975 Kilauea Iki drill core.—Continued

Field no.	75-1-133.4	75-1-141.9	75-1-143.8	75-3-100.9	75-3-106.0	75-3-123.2	75-3-144.4
Lab. no.	D-103856	D-103859	D-103860	D-103873	D-103874	D-103839	D-103877
Job no.	CD53	CE76	CD53	CE76	CE76	CE76	CE76
MgO wt %	10.65	11.62	12.15	9.12	7.98	8.71	16.20
Sc ppm	31.1	29.9	30.4	32.4	33.8	32.7	27.4
Cr ppm	730	877	947	539	398	467	1216
Co ppm	54.1	55.3	57.3	52.3	47.1	47.7	72.2
Ni ppm	349	380	416	190	126	177	664
Zn ppm	101	92	96	110	105	103.9	94
As ppm	<0.7	<0.9	<0.8	<1	1.5	<0.8	<1.1
Se ppm	<3	<2	<3	<3	<2	<2	<2
Rb ppm	12.2	12.4	12.0	15.4	13.6	10.8	9.5
Sr ppm	420	418	441	435	420	465	393
Zr ppm	<500	168	210	157	<300	210	104
Mo ppm	<2	<5	<5	<6	<5	<5	<5
Sb ppm	0.089	<0.1	<0.09	0.14	0.122	<0.08	<0.08
Cs ppm	<0.2	<0.2	<0.2	<0.2	<0.3	<0.3	<0.2
Ba ppm	161	130	129	140	153	142	106
La ppm	16.8	15.2	14.3	16.7	16.7	16.0	11.9
Ce ppm	39.3	36.3	33.8	39.0	38.5	36.9	29.2
Nd ppm	23.2	20.0	19.7	22.6	21.8	21.3	15.4
Sm ppm	6.31	5.69	5.38	6.25	6.27	6.06	4.49
Eu ppm	1.94	1.80	1.68	1.97	2.00	1.91	1.42
Tb ppm	0.93	0.86	0.79	0.92	0.89	0.90	0.679
Yb ppm	2.07	1.78	1.72	2.00	2.00	1.96	1.53
Lu ppm	0.262	0.242	0.231	0.263	0.294	0.262	0.207
Hf ppm	4.23	3.78	3.63	4.40	4.27	4.11	3.00
Ta ppm	1.44	1.29	1.22	1.43	1.45	1.34	1.00
Au ppb	<5	<1	<1	<6	<6	<3	<4
Th ppm	1.39	1.21	1.10	1.37	1.40	1.22	0.93
U ppm	0.40	0.36	0.34	0.32	0.47	0.38	0.26
Type of sample		(III)	(III)	(III)			
Contains glass?	yes	yes	yes	no	no	no	yes
Quenching temperature	high	high	high	low	low	medium	high

Table A4. Instrumental neutron-activation analyses of trace elements for samples from the 1979 Kilauea Iki drill core.

[Most major-element analyses are in Helz and others (1994). wt %, weight percent; ppm, parts per million; nd, not determined; <, less than]

Field no.	79-1R1-167.8	79-1R1-170.8	79-3-145.1	79-3-150.4	79-3-158.0	79-3-160.3	79-3-172.8	79-3R2-168
Lab. no.	W-235378	W-235379	W-210495	W-210496	W-214317	W-210497	W-210500	W-235391
Job no.	CG74	CG74	CD53	CD53	CD53	CE76	CD53	CG74
MgO wt %	3.42	3.48	26.16	13.51	4.5	16.05	18.71	5.07
Sc ppm	21.6	22.0	19.4	30.6	28.8	27.19	26.2	30.1
Cr ppm	9.3	8.8	1280	1108	28.6	1086	1300	37.8
Co ppm	26.4	27.5	114.4	61.8	35.0	73.2	81.7	36.9
Ni ppm	20	33	1280	507	64	684	814	79
Zn ppm	150	152	111	97	133	100	102	138
As ppm	<3	<2	<0.6	<4	<0.8	<1	<0.6	1.16
Se ppm	nd	nd	<2	<2	<3	<3	<2	nd
Rb ppm	36.0	35.1	<8	8.9	27.2	8.8	8.2	24.7
Sr ppm	435	493	<400	410	510	374	290	441
Zr ppm	430	401	<140	170	330	160	<160	276
Mo ppm	4.6	<4	<2	<4	3.9	<5	<6	<4
Sb ppm	0.49	0.19	<0.06	0.145	0.088	<0.1	<0.07	0.17
Cs ppm	0.313	0.36	<0.2	<0.2	<0.2	<0.2	<0.2	<0.3
Ba ppm	389	395	68	122	331	117	88	248
La ppm	50.1	50.3	6.55	12.6	37.3	12.4	10.42	30.8
Ce ppm	112.1	110.2	17.7	31.4	84.1	30.1	26.8	9.9
Nd ppm	61.1	58.4	8.7	18.1	48.8	17.3	14.9	40.2
Sm ppm	16.7	16.3	2.53	4.84	12.2	4.74	4.01	11.04
Eu ppm	4.66	4.60	0.86	1.54	3.69	1.468	1.32	3.24
Tb ppm	2.24	2.23	0.41	0.72	1.77	0.705	0.58	1.55
Yb ppm	4.89	4.78	0.88	1.59	3.96	1.54	1.33	3.41
Lu ppm	0.64	0.63	0.123	0.220	0.540	0.197	0.190	0.43
Hf ppm	11.31	11.24	1.83	3.36	9.07	3.25	2.69	7.59
Ta ppm	3.49	3.53	0.64	1.12	2.95	1.09	0.89	2.63
Au ppb	<9	<11	<4	<7	<6	<12	11.4	34
Th ppm	4.12	4.02	0.49	1.01	3.20	0.99	0.84	2.50
U ppm	1.16	1.11	0.19	0.35	0.84	0.27	0.26	0.71
Type of sample	ooze	ooze	vorb	(III)	segregation vein	(IV)	(IV)	ooze
Contains glass?	yes	yes	trace?	no	yes	yes	yes	yes?
Quenching temperature	high	high	medium	medium	high	high	high	medium

Table A4. Instrumental neutron-activation analyses of trace elements for samples from the 1979 Kilauea Iki drill core.—Continued

Field no.	79-5-160. 0		79-5-163	79-5-180.5	79-5-200.0	79-5-240.0	79-5-260.0	79-5-300.5	79-5-313.5
Lab. no.	W-214304		---------	W-214305	W-214306	W-214308	W-214309	W-214311	W-214313
	a	b							
Job no.	CE76	CE76	CE76	CE76	CE76	CE76	CD53	CE76	CE76
MgO (wt %)	22.08	22.08	2.57	20.7	21.30	20.35	18.84	16.61	9.51
Sc ppm	23.9	23.6	12.5	24.8	23.1	24.8	25.3	26.5	32.7
Cr ppm	1560	1573	24.3	1610	1491	1455	1220	1216	555
Co ppm	93.6	93.2	18.3	87.0	90.8	88.9	81.7	74.2	53.3
Ni ppm	1007	986	65	915	965	923	854	706	226
Zn ppm	100	96	104	98	99	105	99	100	111
As ppm	<1	0.94	2.5	<0.8	1.2	<0.9	<0.7	1.8	<2
Se ppm	<3	<0.8	2.1	<3	<3	<3	<1	<2	<5
Rb ppm	9.1	10.9	62.0	8.3	10.3	<6	7.4	10.8	11.6
Sr ppm	<400	398	<400	<400	<400	438	406	450	<400
Zr ppm	<200	670	119	<220	132	118	130	230	<210
Mo ppm	<6	<5	5.8	<7	<3	<6	2.2	4.7	2.1
Sb ppm	<0.1	<0.08	0.27	<0.09	0.130	<0.1	<0.08	0.10	<0.1
Cs ppm	<0.3	<0.2	0.58	<0.2	<0.2	<0.2	<0.2	0.36	<0.3
Ba ppm	74	97	614	81	83	88	110	102	155
La ppm	8.4	8.5	72.4	9.19	8.99	8.98	11.7	12.6	15.5
Ce ppm	22.6	21.3	161	23.0	23.4	22.11	29.5	29.9	36.4
Nd ppm	11.8	12.1	89.0	11.8	11.6	14.0	15.4	14.7	21.7
Sm ppm	3.27	3.26	21.7	3.53	3.42	3.48	4.36	4.68	5.85
Eu ppm	1.034	1.03	5.51	1.15	1.12	1.17	1.39	1.46	1.84
Tb ppm	0.505	0.499	2.87	0.54	0.518	0.52	0.662	0.76	0.84
Yb ppm	1.07	1.12	6.67	1.21	1.15	1.23	1.46	1.59	1.91
Lu ppm	0.142	0.142	0.880	0.159	0.150	0.156	0.194	0.205	0.264
Hf ppm	2.13	2.10	15.64	2.32	2.40	2.34	3.00	3.16	3.94
Ta ppm	0.69	0.70	4.18	0.769	0.768	0.82	1.00	1.05	1.35
Au ppb	5.3	<3	4.80	0.74	0.77	0.66	0.94	0.92	1.22
U ppm	<0.4	0.22	1.96	<0.4	0.23	<0.4	0.31	0.72	0.38
Type of sample			thin vein				chill	chill	chill
Contains glass?	---no---		yes	trace	trace	no	no	no	no
Quenching temperature	medium		high	high	high	medium	medium	medium	medium

34

Table A5. Instrumental neutron-activation analyses of trace elements from the 1981 Kilauea Iki drill core.

Field no.	81-1-117.8	81-1-119.2	81-1-119.2R	81-1-120.3	81-1-169.9	81-1-190.1	81-1-200.4	81-1-210.0
Lab. no.	W-239453	W-239454		W-239455	W-214102	W-214104	W-214105	W-214106
Job no.	CG74	CE92	CG74	CE92	CD53	CD53	CE76	CE76
MgO (wt %)	4.86	6.74	6.74	6.95	26.87	21.91	25.96	24.53
Sc ppm	30.5	30.1	31.3	30.3	18.3	23.4	19.4	22.1
Cr ppm	11.0	320	332	370	1252	1468	1474	1700
Co ppm	40.5	38.5	38.5	39.5	119.9	94.2	112.6	103.4
Ni ppm	62	143	139	140	1290	1001	1260	1150
Zn ppm	144	82.7	105	86	118	105	110	99
As ppm	<2	<0.7	<1	1.4	<0.8	<0.6	1.02	<0.9
Se ppm	nd	nd	nd	nd	<2	<0.9	<0.9	<0.9
Rb ppm	22.6	16.2	14.3	15.7	7.1	11.4	10.8	<6.0
Sr ppm	432	484	442	450	260	289	<400	<500
Zr ppm	266	<400	163	204	<150	141	<200	<200
Mo ppm	<7	<5	3.8	3.4	<6	<6	<7	<7
Sb ppm	<0.2	<0.08	0.24	0.14	<0.08	<0.07	0.409	<0.2
Cs ppm	0.23	<0.2	<0.2	<0.2	<0.3	<0.2	<0.2	<0.2
Ba ppm	290	163	185	159	77	88	74	61
La ppm	29.3	19.3	20.1	18.8	8.0	9.1	8.48	6.6
Ce ppm	65.3	43.4	45.3	41.7	20.4	22.3	20.8	16.3
Nd ppm	37.1	25.1	26.2	24.3	11.0	11.9	12.6	9.3
Sm ppm	10.30	6.81	7.43	6.62	2.94	3.45	3.12	2.57
Eu ppm	3.10	2.20	2.26	2.17	0.91	1.10	0.99	0.850
Tb ppm	1.46	1.08	1.043	1.029	0.443	0.535	0.44	0.418
Yb ppm	3.30	2.35	2.40	2.22	1.06	1.13	1.05	0.85
Lu ppm	0.431	0.310	0.305	0.298	0.130	0.147	0.147	0.118
Hf ppm	7.42	4.88	5.02	4.65	2.04	2.23	2.13	1.69
Ta ppm	2.64	1.68	1.73	1.60	0.71	0.788	0.67	0.522
Au ppb	<9	<5	<3	<5	<1	<5	<6	6.6
Th ppm	2.41	1.63	1.69	1.47	0.60	0.71	0.77	0.53
U ppm	0.65	0.40	0.38	0.52	0.26	0.29	<0.3	0.23
Type of sample	(II)	(II)	(II)	(II)	vorb	(V)	ogb	(V)
Contains glass?	no	no	no	no	yes	yes	yes	yes
Quenching temperature	low	low	low	low	high	high	high	high

Table A5. Instrumental neutron-activation analyses of trace elements from the 1981 Kilauea Iki drill core.— Continued

Field no.	81-1-230.6	81-1-239.9	81-1-250.0	81-1-260.0	81-1-270.2	81-1-273.6	81-1-273.6R	81-1-280.0
Lab. no.	W-214108	W-214109	W-214110	W-214111	W-214112	W-214113		W-214114
Job no.	CD53	CE76	CE76	CD53	CE76	CD53	CG74	CD53
MgO wt%	24.83	26.55	25.43	22.77	18.79	11.95	11.95	26.15
Sc ppm	22.2	20.0	20.8	23.8	27.8	32.8	32.0	20.8
Cr ppm	1770	1820	1730	1620	1329	982	948	1900
Co ppm	102.4	111.2	105.7	97.5	84.2	54.5	2.3	106.6
Ni ppm	1210	1310	1250	1110	752	336	356	1320
Zn ppm	98	96	98	101	86	89	84	91
As ppm	<0.8	0.91	<0.9	<0.6	<0.9	<0.9	<1	<0.6
Se ppm	<0.9	<2	<0.7	3.5	<0.8	<4	nd	<0.9
Rb ppm	6.1	8.1	<6	7.6	<7	7.9	9.6	7.0
Sr ppm	<400	<300	<400	262	380	420	386	220
Zr ppm	<90	<110	<100	<90	<110	111	<230	<150
Mo ppm	<6	<5	<6	<5	<6	<3	<4	<6
Sb ppm	<0.08	<0.9	<0.1	0.093	<0.2	<0.09	<0.1	<0.07
Cs ppm	<0.2	<0.2	<0.2	<0.2	<0.2	<0.2	<0.2	<0.2
Ba ppm	66	66	73	67	86	100	93	58
La ppm	6.3	5.98	6.27	7.00	5.27	9.29	9.2	6.34
Ce ppm	17.5	14.8	14.5	18.4	13.3	22.5	21.9	17.3
Nd ppm	9.8	9.0	7.9	9.0	8.0	12.6	12.9	8.1
Sm ppm	2.50	2.35	2.49	2.75	2.41	3.77	3.74	2.51
Eu ppm	0.80	0.786	0.86	0.915	0.855	1.27	1.28	0.85
Tb ppm	0.381	0.36	0.397	0.422	0.40	0.550	0.572	0.422
Yb ppm	0.86	0.80	0.87	0.98	0.86	1.29	1.24	0.85
Lu ppm	0.115	0.106	0.111	0.132	0.106	0.168	0.159	0.120
Hf ppm	1.52	1.56	1.60	1.87	1.48	2.44	2.37	1.58
Ta ppm	0.518	0.490	0.580	0.597	0.463	0.718	0.755	0.536
Au ppb	<4	<0.7	<5	<0.9	<2	<9	<2	<4
Th ppm	0.46	0.43	0.46	0.49	0.32	0.61	0.69	0.46
U ppm	0.37	<0.3	0.17	0.29	<0.4	<0.3	0.21	0.57
Type of sample	(V)	(V)	(V)	(V)	(VI)	(VI)	(VI)	(VI)
Contains glass?	yes	yes	yes	yes	yes	yes	yes	yes
Quenching temperature	high	high	high	high	high	high	high	high

Table A5. Instrumental neutron-activation analyses of trace elements from the 1981 Kilauea Iki drill core.—Continued

Field no.	81-1-281.6	81-1-289.3	81-1-297.9	81-1-300.2	81-1-306.7	81-2-88.6
Lab. no.	W-214115	W-214116	W-214118	W-214119	W-214120	W-232725
Job no.	CD53	CE76	CE76	CD53	CD53	CD53
MgO wt %	18.74	25.58	15.64	18.15	17.47	2.37
Sc ppm	25.7	19.5	27.0	25.7	26.4	18.8
Cr ppm	1329	1581	1102	1133	1150	1.9
Co ppm	83.9	107.2	71.0	81.5	78.7	23.6
Ni ppm	832	1270	628	801	729	<30
Zn ppm	104	102	94	104	99	164
As ppm	<0.9	0.85	<1	<0.7	<1.1	1.73
Se ppm	<1.8	<0.7	<2.9	<3.2	<0.9	<4
Rb ppm	7.1	9.1	11.4	8.2	9.3	48.1
Sr ppm	320	<290	410	370	409	500
Zr ppm	149	<100	110	81	148	580
Mo ppm	<6	<6	<4	<3	<6	4.8
Sb ppm	<0.09	<0.08	<0.1	<0.07	<0.09	0.24
Cs ppm	0.35	<0.2	<0.2	<0.2	<0.2	0.36
Ba ppm	116	<90	117	116	100	518
La ppm	11.6	5.90	11.5	11.8	10.4	63.6
Ce ppm	28.1	14.7	27.6	28.6	26.0	142.9
Nd ppm	16.3	8.2	15.4	16.1	14.1	82.3
Sm ppm	4.35	2.32	4.42	4.41	4.01	20.7
Eu ppm	1.35	0.769	1.41	1.39	1.35	5.59
Tb ppm	0.631	0.368	0.658	0.670	0.585	2.79
Yb ppm	1.37	0.84	1.56	1.45	1.29	6.18
Lu ppm	0.187	0.115	0.193	0.191	0.184	0.813
Hf ppm	2.88	1.44	2.95	2.88	2.63	14.37
Ta ppm	1.03	0.47	0.95	1.00	0.88	4.16
Au ppb	<1	<1	<2	<5	<9	<8
Th ppm	0.90	0.45	0.93	0.94	0.79	5.31
U ppm	0.24	<0.3	<0.4	0.33	0.27	1.51
Type of sample	leopard rock	(V) septum	foundered crust	leopard rock	deepest core	vein in vein
Contains glass?	yes	yes	yes	yes	yes	no
Quenching temperature	high	high	high	high	high	low

Table A6. Instrumental neutron-activation analyses of trace elements from the 1988 Kilauea Iki drill core.
[Major-element analyses are in Helz and Taggart (2010). wt %, weight percent; ppm, parts per million; <, less than]

Field no.	88-1-198.6	88-1-234.4	88-1-260.0	88-1-268.5	88-1-277.8	88-1-311.6	88-1-371.2	88-1-375.8
Lab. no.	W-256765	W-256737	W-256739	W-256739	W-256740	W-256743	W-256748	W-256749
Job no.	CJ13	CJ12	CJ12	CJ12	CJ12	CJ12	CJ12	CJ12
MgO wt %	22.8	23.8	25.0	23.2	23.2	18.7	18.4	18.3
Sc ppm	23.3	23.2	20.8	20.9	23.3	24.6	25.3	25.0
Cr ppm	1660	1670	1590	1337	1650	1211	1263	1224
Co ppm	93.5	95.1	101.4	92.8	94.4	78.5	77.9	77.9
Ni ppm	1010	1020	1170	1090	1010	778	778	764
Zn ppm	88	86	93	93.5	86	85	87	93
As ppm	<0.4	<0.3	0.61	<0.4	<0.4	<0.5	<0.5	0.85
Se ppm	<0.6	<0.7	<0.6	<0.5	<2	<0.6	<0.7	<0.7
Rb ppm	5.8	6.6	6	9.5	<5	9.2	8	11.4
Sr ppm	255	291	217	254	244	320	310	314
Zr ppm	<100	<140	92	91	<120	<140	103	<200
Mo ppm	<2	<3	<3	<4	<3	<5	<4	<4
Sb ppm	0.17	<0.05	0.101	0.126	0.083	0.147	0.46	0.174
Cs ppm	<0.1	<0.1	<0.1	<0.1	<0.1	<0.1	0.16	0.17
Ba ppm	62	58	65	78	54	100	104	95
La ppm	7.51	6.69	6.61	9.05	6.36	11.7	11.6	11.4
Ce ppm	16.9	14.9	15.5	20.5	14.7	25.5	26.0	25.6
Nd ppm	10.1	9.7	8.7	11.6	8.8	16.7	15.9	15.8
Sm ppm	2.96	2.65	2.62	3.43	2.58	4.33	4.44	4.34
Eu ppm	0.973	0.912	0.876	1.11	0.891	1.41	1.39	1.37
Tb ppm	0.443	0.397	0.378	0.48	0.378	0.661	0.661	0.636
Yb ppm	1.00	0.86	0.83	1.05	0.90	1.31	1.40	1.37
Lu ppm	0.121	0.111	0.107	0.153	0.123	0.192	0.189	0.188
Hf ppm	1.93	1.82	1.64	2.28	1.68	2.91	2.95	2.99
Ta ppm	0.628	0.55	0.54	0.75	0.542	0.966	0.976	0.98
Au ppb	<4	<3	<5	<3	<4	<5	<3	<3
Th ppm	0.64	0.52	0.53	0.79	0.5	1.01	0.95	0.97
U ppm	0.21	0.16	<0.2	0.28	<0.2	0.3	0.3	0.36
Type of sample	(V)	(V)	(V)	speckled rock body	(V)	(VII)	deepest core	
Contains glass?	no	no	yes	yes	yes	no	no	no
Quenching temperature	low	medium	high	high	high	high	medium	medium

Table A6. Instrumental neutron-activation analyses of trace elements from the 1988 Kilauea Iki drill core.—Continued

Field no.	88-2-215.8		88-2-256.4	88-2-276.3	88-2-301.7	88-2-322.3	88-2-348.5	88-2-354.9
Lab. no.	W-256722		W-256725	W256727	W-256729	W-256731	W-256734	W-256735
	a	b						
Job no.	CJ12	CJ12	CJ12	CJ12	CJ12	CJ12	CJ12	CJ12
MgO wt %	24.3	24.3	23.4	20.8	22.1	15.6	15.7	18.2
Sc ppm	22.4	22.4	21.8	23.2	22.9	27.9	26.3	25.3
Cr ppm	1690	1650	1521	1353	1520	1184	940	1199
Co ppm	97.3	96.4	96.0	86.8	89.7	68.8	70.9	77.4
Ni ppm	1090	1060	1000	890	930	541	617	752
Zn ppm	85	81.5	94	90	93.9	86	94	88
As ppm	<0.3	<0.4	<0.3	<0.4	<0.4	<0.5	<0.6	<0.5
Se ppm	<1	<0.8	<0.6	<0.5	<0.6	<0.7	<0.7	<0.7
Rb ppm	7.1	8.1	8.1	<10	<13	<10	11.0	8.9
Sr ppm	244	240	262	290	267	347	378	290
Zr ppm	83	73	<180	90	65	<100	132	110
Mo ppm	6	<3	<3	<4	<3	<4	<5	<3
Sb ppm	0.15	0.37	0.129	0.114	0.160	0.091	<0.2	0.108
Cs ppm	<0.1	<0.1	<0.1	<0.1	<0.1	<0.1	<0.1	<0.2
Ba ppm	63	57	67	<100	48	80	110	108
La ppm	6.63	6.65	6.97	7.62	4.93	6.71	12.7	11.5
Ce ppm	14.5	15.2	15.2	16.9	11.8	15.6	28.3	25.5
Nd ppm	9.4	8.8	9.2	10.3	7.6	9.8	18.1	14.9
Sm ppm	2.68	2.69	2.72	3.02	2.21	2.88	4.81	4.38
Eu ppm	0.865	0.898	0.925	1.028	0.825	1.15	1.55	1.41
Tb ppm	0.416	0.399	0.404	0.453	0.353	0.45	0.721	0.64
Yb ppm	0.89	0.89	0.89	0.99	0.75	0.98	1.54	1.50
Lu ppm	0.12	0.12	0.124	0.130	0.112	0.141	0.215	0.188
Hf ppm	1.70	1.83	1.81	1.94	1.29	1.88	3.27	2.91
Ta ppm	0.564	0.561	0.55	0.6	0.38	0.61	1.12	1.01
Au ppb	<3	<3	<3	<3	<3	<4	<4	<3
Th ppm	0.52	0.48	0.59	0.59	0.40	0.46	1.06	0.92
U ppm	0.140	0.152	0.149	0.211	0.088	0.19	0.28	0.29
Type of sample	----(V)----		(V)	(VI)	(VI)	(VII)		deepest core
Contains glass?	no		yes	yes	yes	yes	no	no
Quenching temperature	medium		high	high	high	high	medium	medium

Table B1. Energy-dispersive X-ray fluorescence analyses of trace elements in samples from the 1959 Kilauea Iki eruption.

[Major-element analyses are as in table A1. Mixing fractions are from Wright (1973). wt %, weight percent; ppm, parts per million; °C, degrees Celsius; <, less than]

Field no.	Iki-1	Iki-58	Iki-22	Iki-3	Iki-44	Iki-38
Lab. no.	S-2	S-1	S-5	D-571089	S-7	S-25
Job no.	CH91	CH91	CH91	CH91	CH91	CH91
MgO (wt%)	7.23	8.08	19.52	17.2	13.67	8.85
Nb ppm	23	23	15	21	21	19
Rb ppm	16	12	<10	16	14	14
Sr ppm	385	365	275	300	335	370
Zr ppm	184	176	130	142	158	178
Y ppm	28	31	23	32	27	32
Cu ppm	122	124	120	102	114	144
Ni ppm	112	130	790	610	480	240
Zn ppm	100	102	104	96	114	112
Phase of eruption	1	1	1	1	1	17
Fraction S-1/(S-1+S+2)	0	1	0.68	0.75	0.057	0
Quenching temperature (°C)	1142	1144	1217	1213	1187	---

Table B2. Energy-dispersive X-ray fluorescence analyses of trace elements for samples from 1967 Kilauea Iki drill core.

[wt %, weight percent; ppm, parts per million]

Field no.	67-1-89.0	67-2-17.0	67-2-59.8	67-2-79.9	67-2-85.7	67-2-89.5	67-2-94.6	67-3-6.8	67-3-27.5	67-3-39.0	67-3-47.8	67-3-58.0	67-3-87.0
Lab. no.	D-102046	W-214299	W-214301	W-214302	D-102048	D-102050	D-103993	W-214121	D-103976	D-103977	D-103978	D-103979	D-102054
Job no.	CH90	CH90	CH90	CH90	CH90	CH90	CH90	CH91	CH90	CH91	CH91	CH90	CH90
MgO (wt %)	4.83	18.26	16.53	22.34	2.60	13.07	15.91	25.83	12.01	10.73	13.10	8.91	5.44
Nb ppm	37	15	18	16	56	23	16	14	18	21	19	23	33
Rb ppm	21	12	12	15	46	15	11	10	11	11	16	17	21
Sr ppm	405	295	310	255	430	335	305	215	345	365	345	410	415
Zr ppm	305	124	134	104	580	172	122	97	156	172	164	192	285
Y ppm	43	24	26	25	70	31	24	22	27	30	30	33	40
Cu ppm	215	81	102	78	450	140	93	60	86	104	99	100	215
Ni ppm	78	710	600	920	22	440	495	1200	320	265	400	210	79
Zn ppm	128	95	94	97	152	110	87	90	92	86	90	82	126
Type of sample	glass in bit	(I)	foundered crust	foundered crust	ooze	leopard rock	foundered crust	(I)	(I)	(I)	(II)	(II)	glass in bit
Contains glass?	yes	no	yes	yes	yes	yes	yes	no	no	no	no	no	yes
Quenching temperature	high	low	medium	high	high	high	high	low	low	low	medium	medium	high

Table B3. Energy-dispersive X-ray fluorescence analyses of trace elements for samples from 1975 Kilauea Iki drill core.
[wt %, weight percent; ppm, parts per million]

Field no.	75-1-60.9	75-1-75.2	75-1-85.5	75-1-95.0	75-1-110	75-1-114.9	75-1-121.5	75-1-133.4	75-1-141.9	75-3-100.9	75-3-106.0	75-3-123.2	75-3-144.4
Lab. No.	D-103844	D-103846	D-103848	D-103850	D-103852	D-103853	D-103855	D-103856	D-103859	D-103873	D-103874	D-103839	D-103877
Job no.	CH91	CH91	CH91	CH90	CH90	CH90	CH91	CH91	CH90	CH90	CH90	CH90	CH90
MgO (wt %)	10.52	5.77	8.33	9.64	8.27	5.26	7.77	10.65	11.62	9.12	7.98	8.71	16.20
Nb ppm	21	25	20	21	22	34	22	24	21	20	23	20	16
Rb ppm	16	18	11	12	16	26	19	14	11	19	17	16	14
Sr ppm	385	450	410	400	410	465	430	375	350	375	400	390	305
Zr ppm	182	240	184	170	190	295	198	178	164	180	186	172	136
Y ppm	32	38	32	31	32	47	37	32	29	32	32	30	28
Cu ppm	106	168	118	110	122	190	138	104	114	92	124	114	102
Ni ppm	260	72	180	230	180	57	146	280	330	158	110	154	540
Zn ppm	85	89	77	79	79	91	73	85	87	81	80	78	90
Type of sample	(II)	segregation vein	(II)	(II)	(II)	segregation vein	(II)	(III)	(III)				
Contains glass?	no	no	no	no	no	no	no	yes	yes	no	no	no	yes
Quenching temperature	low	low	low	low	medium	medium	medium	high	high	low	low	medium	high

42

Table B4. Energy-dispersive X-ray fluorescence analyses of trace elements for samples from 1979 Kilauea Iki core.

[wt %, weight percent; ppm, parts per million; <, less than]

Field no. Lab. no. Job no.	79-1R1-167.8 W-235378 CH90	79-1R1-170.9 W-235380 CH90	79-3-145.1 W-210495 CH91	79-3-150.4 W-210496 CH91	79-3-158.0 W-214317 CH91	79-3-160.3 W-210497 CH90	79-3-172.8 W-210500 CH91	79-3R2-168.0 W-235391 CH90	79-5-160.0 W-214304 CH90	79-5-163 ---- CH90	79-5-180.5 W-214305 CH90
MgO (wt %)	3.42	3.48	26.16	13.51	4.5	16.05	18.71	5.07	22.08	2.57	20.7
Nb ppm	48	51	13	17	37	16	15	38	13	61	15
Rb ppm	34	35	<10	14	27	<10	<10	21	11	64	<10
Sr ppm	430	430	194	335	440	310	265	410	240	360	255
Zr ppm	480	475	83	144	375	136	118	315	96	680	106
Y ppm	63	61	19	29	51	25	24	45	21	79	23
Cu ppm	210	365	58	102	196	92	93	245	76	640	81
Ni ppm	35	27	1100	405	61	570	700	73	850	31	790
Zn ppm	134	134	112	88	100	95	97	124	96	58	93
Type of sample	Ooze	ooze	vorb	(III)	segregation vein	(IV)	(IV)	ooze		thin vein	
Contains glass?	Yes	yes	trace?	no	yes	yes	yes	yes?	no	yes	trace
Quenching temperature	High	high	medium	medium	high	high	high	medium	medium	high	high

43

Table B4. Energy-dispersive X-ray fluorescence analyses of trace elements for samples from 1979 Kilauea Iki core.—Continued

Field no	79-5-200.0	79-5-240.0	79-5-260.0	79-5-300.5	79-5-313.5
Lab no.	W-214306	W-214308	W-214309	W-214311	W-214313
Job no.	CH90	CH90	CH91	CH90	CH90
MgO (wt %)	21.30	20.35	18.84	16.61	9.51
Nb ppm	13	13	18	16	20
Rb ppm	<10	11	14	12	15
Sr ppm	255	270	290	305	365
Zr ppm	106	104	124	136	172
Y ppm	24	24	28	26	31
Cu ppm	90	94	91	96	108
Ni ppm	800	770	680	610	210
Zn ppm	104	96	87	95	89
Type of sample			chill	chill	chill
Contains glass?	trace	no	no	no	no
Quenching temperature	high	medium	medium	medium	medium

44

Table B5. Energy-dispersive X-ray fluorescence analyses of trace elements from 1981 Kilauea Iki drill core.
[wt %, weight percent; ppm, parts per million; $<$, less than]

Field no.	81-1-117.8	81-1-119.2	81-1-120.3	81-1-169.9	81-1-190.1	81-1-200.4	81-1-210.0	81-1-230.6	81-1-239.9	81-1-250.0	81-1-260.0
Lab. no.	W-239453	W-239454	W-239455	W-214102	W-210104	W-214105	W-214106	W-214108	W-214109	W-214110	W-214111
Job no.	CH90	CH91	CH91	CH91	CH91	CH90	CH90	CH91	CH90	CH90	CH91
MgO (wt %)	4.86	6.74	6.95	26.87	21.91	25.96	24.53	24.83	26.55	25.43	22.77
Nb ppm	36	21	24	14	15	13	12	12	10	11	14
Rb ppm	25	14	16	11	13	<10	<10	11	<10	11	<10
Sr ppm	450	440	440	180	240	192	200	205	186	205	230
Zr ppm	305	205	205	97	108	98	80	81	73	83	85
Y ppm	45	33	36	22	24	20	18	19	17	20	18
Cu ppm	220	132	138	70	88	88	63	70	66	67	71
Ni ppm	63	122	128	1100	860	1100	1000	1000	1100	1050	910
Zn ppm	92	72	77	116	96	116	102	99	106	104	97
Type of sample	(II)	(II)	(II)	vorb	(V)	ogb	(V)	(V)	(V)	(V)	(V)
Contains glass?	no	no	no	yes	yes	yes	yes	yes	yes	yes	yes
Quenching temperature	low	low	low	high	high	high	high	high	high	high	high

Table B5. Energy-dispersive X-ray fluorescence analyses of trace elements from 1981 Kilauea Iki drill core.—Continued

	81-1-270.2 W-214112 CH90	81-1-273.6 W-214113 CH91	81-1-280.0 W-214114 CH91	81-1-281.6 W-214115 CH91	81-1-289.3 W-214116 CH90	81-1-297.9 W-214118 CH90	81-1-300.2 W-214119 CH91	81-1-306.7 W-214120 CH91	81-2-88.6 W-232725 CH91
Field no. Lab no. Job no.									
MgO (wt %)	18.79	11.95	26.15	18.74	25.58	15.64	18.15	17.47	2.37
Nb ppm	10	14	10	17	11	16	18	14	55
Rb ppm	<10	<10	<10	12	<10	10	15	<10	43
Sr ppm	260	350	200	275	205	310	285	295	430
Zr ppm	76	108	80	132	75	132	132	118	590
Y ppm	18	23	19	24	18	23	23	23	70
Cu ppm	50	70	67	102	64	102	98	92	345
Ni ppm	620	290	1100	710	1100	530	650	630	<10
Zn ppm	88	75	97	98	106	93	102	92	108
Type of sample	(VI)	(VI)	(VI)	leopard rock	(V) septum	foundered crust	leopard rock	deepest core	vein in vein
Contains glass?	yes	yes	yes	yes	yes	yes	yes	yes	no
Quenching temperature	high	high	high	high	high	high	high	high	low

46